Chaos, Management and Economics:

The Implications of Non-Linear Thinking

DAVID PARKER
University of Birmingham

and

RALPH STACEY
University of Hertfordshire

IEA

Published by
INSTITUTE OF ECONOMIC AFFAIRS
1994

First published in May 1994
Second Impression January 1995
Third Impression December 1997

by

THE INSTITUTE OF ECONOMIC AFFAIRS
2 Lord North Street, Westminster,
London SW1P 3LB

Hobart Paper 125

ISSN 0073-2818

ISBN 0-255 36333-8

Many IEA publications are translated into languages other than
English or are reprinted. Permission to translate or to reprint
should be sought from the Editorial Director at the address above.

Cover design by The Jenkins Group

Printed in Great Britain by
Optichrome The Printing Group, Woking, Surrey
Set in Baskerville 11 on 12 point

CONTENTS

[4]

FOREWORD

In the natural sciences, chaos – a creative state in which order and disorder mingle – is now recognised by many researchers as providing a better explanation of how the world works than the more orderly view which used to prevail. As Dr David Parker and Professor Ralph Stacey explain in Hobart Paper 125, the concepts of 'chaos theory' can also be fruitfully applied to economic and social systems. The implications for the management of business and for the management of the economy are profound.

A chaotic world is more complex than can be captured by the linear equations generally used by economic modellers and by the conventional analyses of management scientists. In Parker and Stacey's words:

> 'A simple view of how the world works is being replaced by an essentially complex and paradoxical one' (p.11).

In this world, links between cause and effect are extremely complex. Disequilibrium is the norm rather than an aberration. Indeed, disequilibrium is a creative state which generates not only threats but opportunities which can be seized by the entrepreneurs through whose efforts economic progress occurs.

A particularly interesting feature of this *Hobart Paper* to many IEA readers will be that, as Parker and Stacey acknowledge, the disequilibrium world they describe bears a striking similarity to the view taken by economists of the Austrian School. Chaos theory is compatible with

> '...the methodology and policy prescriptions of Austrian economics with its themes of spontaneous self-organisation, enterprise and creative destruction' (p.94)

rather than with neo-classical economics which emphasises equilibrium states. Moreover, Parker and Stacey's conclusions (set out in Chapter V) are very similar to those which most 'Austrians' would support, even though those conclusions are reached by a very different route.

Among Dr Parker and Professor Stacey's conclusions are the following. The long-term future is inherently unknowable; economies which '...cope best with chaotic conditions are likely to be those which promote entrepreneurial adaptation' (p.93); small errors in demand management may lead to increased economic instability; attempts by governments or companies at '...conscious design or planning of long-term futures will inevitably break down' (p.93); firms and economies most likely to succeed are those '...which are open to change and at the same time can contain the resulting social and economic tensions' (p.94).

The views expressed in this *Hobart Paper* are those of the authors, not of the Institute (which has no corporate view), its Trustees, Directors or Advisers. It is published as a clear explanation of chaos theory and its implications for managers and economists which, as its authors say, 'provides a new and exciting departure point for the study of organisations and economies' (p.95).

May 1994   COLIN ROBINSON
Editorial Director, Institute of Economic Affairs;
Professor of Economics, University of Surrey

THE AUTHORS

DAVID PARKER, PhD, lectures in managerial and international economics in the Department of Commerce at the University of Birmingham. He received his doctorate from the Cranfield School of Management.

He has lectured in a number of UK universities and was a visiting senior researcher at the University of York and the University of Naples. He has contributed widely to journals and books on economics and management. Recent books include *The Essence of the Economy* (1990) and *The Essence of Business Economics* (1992), both published by Prentice Hall, and *Profit and Enterprise: the Political Economy of Profit* (1991), published by Harvester Wheatsheaf.

He has acted as a consultant for a number of private and public sector organisations and is an executive director of two publishing companies in the North-east of England.

RALPH STACEY, PhD, is Professor of Strategic Management at the Business School, University of Hertfordshire, and is a visiting lecturer at Vaxjo University, Sweden. His doctorate was awarded by the London School of Economics.

He is the author of a number of books on management, including *The Chaos Frontier: Creative Strategic Control for Business* (1991), Butterworth/Heinemann, *Dynamic Strategic Management for the 1990s* (1990), Kogan Page, *Strategic Management and Organisational Dynamics* (1993), Pitman Publishing, and *Managing Chaos* (1992), Kogan Page.

Before entering teaching, he worked as an investment strategist and was the Corporate Planning Manager at John Laing plc. He continues to maintain consulting links with a number of major corporations.

I. INTRODUCTION: A CHAOTIC WORLD

'Now, my suspicion is that the universe is not only queerer than we suppose, but queerer than we can suppose....'

(J.B.S. Haldane, 1928, p.286)

A major revolution is now well advanced in the natural sciences. The way in which scientists understand and explain how the world works is being turned on its head. Previously, they cast their explanations primarily in terms of order and regularity. They saw a world of systems moving in predictable, pre-ordained ways according to deterministic natural laws, in which orderly causes lead to orderly effects. Now, they emphasise the creative rôle of disorder and irregularity. They see a world of systems moving in self-organising ways with emergent and unpredictable outcomes. There are still deterministic natural laws, but they are now understood to operate in a circular way in which disorder leads to order and order leads to disorder. A simple view of how the world works is being replaced by an essentially complex and paradoxical one.

The new science is called non-linear dynamics, or complexity theory, and the aspect of this new science which has attracted the most popular attention is called chaos theory. It is perhaps unfortunate that the new science should have come to be so identified with the term 'chaos' because, in its popular meaning, that word connotes absolute and total muddle, complete mayhem and randomness. This is not, however, what scientists mean by the term. For them, chaos is an intricate mixture of order and disorder, regularity and irregularity: patterns of behaviour which are irregular but are nevertheless recognisable as broad categories of behaviour, or archetypes, within which there is endless individual variety. You only have to watch the clouds for a short while to understand what scientists mean by chaotic behaviour.

The ubiquity of such chaos in human affairs is intuitively recognised in popular sayings such as: 'History always repeats itself but never in the same way twice.' The purpose of this *Hobart Paper* is to explore that intuitive recognition, and to

[11]

examine how the new science of complexity and chaos might give us a deeper insight into how human organisations and economies function. We can certainly do with all the new insights we can get, bearing in mind how difficult managers seem to find it to design and sustain creative organisations and how much difficulty governments have in carrying out effective economic and social policies.

Linearity and Non-Linearity

To put the task to be undertaken in this *Hobart Paper* into perspective, consider first the sense in which the new science of complexity is a revolution for both the natural and social sciences.

Traditionally, both natural and social scientists have explained the behaviour of systems in linear terms. They knew, of course, that the true relationships were non-linear, but non-linear relationships are notoriously difficult to handle and it was generally held to be a useful and acceptable simplification to employ linear approximations (Pesaran and Potter (eds.), 1993, p.vii). To see whether such a simplification is in practice useful and acceptable, reflect for a moment on the differences between linear and non-linear systems.

First, in a linear relationship a given cause has one and only one effect, a given action has one and only one outcome. But in a non-linear relationship, a given cause or action can have many different effects or outcomes. In other words, linear equations have only one solution and they can normally be easily solved; but non-linear equations have more than one solution and there is no general method of solving most of them.

Second, linear systems have a simple additive property in that they are the sum of their components. You can break a linear system up into its components, study and explain each component, then put it all back together again and you will have an explanation of the whole. Non-linear systems do not have this simple additive property. They exhibit synergy in the sense that they are more than the sum of their components. You cannot therefore fully understand a non-linear system by the reductionist method of breaking it apart and then putting it back together. Instead, you have to adopt a holistic or systemic approach in which you try to understand

[12]

the patterns of behaviour which the system as a whole produces.

Given these differences it is acceptable and useful to employ a linear approximation of a non-linear system only if the following conditions hold. Synergy has to be relatively unimportant and some method has to be devised of taking into account both this minimal synergy and the range of effects which a single cause might have. The standard method of doing this is to use probability theory in statistics. All the relationships in the system to be studied are assumed to be stochastic and 'error' terms are introduced into them. These error terms are intended to take care of any misspecification of the relationships, any relationships omitted and any random shocks to the system. This theory in statistics, built on assumptions about how these errors are distributed and with variances that are finite, enables scientists to estimate stochastic, linear approximations of non-linear relationships.

This approach works if the error terms are distributed as statistical theory assumes them to be, if variances are indeed finite, and if some tiny error, some 'noise' in the system, does not escalate and take over, to alter completely the behaviour of the system. Large random shocks will have major effects, but tiny unnoticeable errors which we cannot hope to measure can safely be ignored. For centuries, scientists in both the natural and the social disciplines have made just such, often unquestioned, assumptions.

The revolution mentioned earlier lies in the discovery that these assumptions are usually not valid. It is now understood that non-linear feedback systems are highly sensitive to initial conditions, which means that some tiny error to a number of decimal places, some imperceptible 'noise' in the system, can escalate into major qualitative changes in the behaviour of that system. In such systems we cannot safely assume that small errors are unimportant. Errors are not distributed in the way statistical theory assumes; instead, variances are infinite so that standard estimation techniques break down. The range of effects to which a single cause can lead may well be huge. In fact, the links between cause and effect disappear in the complexity of interactions. In consequence, the long-term future of the system is inherently unpredictable. In such systems, a butterfly taking flight in Tokyo may trigger a hurricane in New York and nobody will be able to trace the steps back from the hurricane to the butterfly. Nobody will ever be sure what caused the hurricane. In such systems, synergy becomes all-important. We have to understand behaviour in systemic, holistic terms rather than reductionist, causal ones.

Chaos and the Long-Term Future

The implications of this discovery are indeed revolutionary. In the presence of sensitivity to initial conditions, the purpose of science can no longer be detailed prediction. Instead, its purpose becomes that of explaining and understanding (Gleick, 1988; Waldrop, 1994). Systems which demonstrate *sensitive dependence on initial conditions** will not be successfully engineered or planned. They cannot be controlled through monitoring their performance against some standard. They cannot be driven to realise anyone's prior intention. Instead, such systems evolve through a process of self-organisation from which their futures emerge. Members of such a system contribute to its unfolding future, but none can be in control of it.

Clearly, if human systems are of this type, it will be impossible to engineer or plan their long-term futures successfully. Consider what it means to plan the long-term future of a system. It means that those members of the system who wish to control it must agree on some specification of the long-term future of that system they want. Then they must agree on some sequence of actions they are going to pursue to realise their shared intention. Next, they must act together and keep reviewing the outcomes of their actions against their intentions, taking corrective action to remove any serious divergences. People can follow this procedure whenever they like, of course, but such procedures will be *effective* only if the desired future state can somehow be linked back to the actions required to realise it. If, however, the link between action and long-term outcome is lost, that is, if the long-term future is inherently unpredictable, as scientists now say it is for creative non-linear systems, then any long-term planning procedures followed will simply not achieve the desired outcome, except occasionally by chance. Instead of

---

* Words and phrases set in italics and followed by an asterisk are defined/explained in the 'Glossary', below, pp. 96-97.

[14]

relying on long-term plans, creative managers and policy-makers will have to rely on a self-organising process of organisational learning from which futures emerge unpredictably without prior shared intention. The future will be determined not by prior intentions and plans but by the detailed manner in which institutions evolve.

Short-Term Planning

Each of the statements above about planning procedures has been qualified by the words 'long term'. In the kinds of non-linear systems we are discussing it takes time for small changes to escalate into major consequences. It follows that the short-term behaviour of such a system may be reasonably predictable. It is, therefore, possible to plan for the short term and the degree of planning success will depend upon the degree of predictability. Indeed, we 'planned' yesterday to write this text today. You no doubt 'planned' a short while ago to read it. A firm plans to launch a new product this month and does so. The government intends to cut taxes in the forthcoming budget and achieves the reduction (sometimes). We plan to go to work tomorrow and will set our alarm clocks accordingly. We do not wish to question 'planning' when used in this sense of an intended action, or even sometimes of intended short-term outcomes of such actions.

Equally, we have no argument, as such, with the notion of 'scenario planning', as used by companies like Shell (Beck, 1981; Wack, 1985). In such longer-run 'planning', various possible future scenarios relating to production, demand, competition and so on are mapped out and managers practise possible responses. Such scenario planning is not planning at all. It is a form of learning intended to improve skills at responding to events as they occur. What the new science questions is the idea that we can ever usefully plan or intend the long-term outcomes of our actions or that we can always plan short-term outcomes. Sometimes a planned outcome may be achieved, sometimes it will not be. Importantly, there is no means of knowing in advance which will occur. Equally, in terms of scenario planning there is no guarantee that any of the scenarios discussed will prove accurate.

Those who believe the long-term future of economies and firms can be planned will have to abandon their programmes

[15]

if creative human systems are non-linear feedback ones operating close to chaos. The proponents of planning systems will have to limit their approach to managing and controlling the short-term outcomes of existing day-to-day activities of organisations and economies – that is, to the planning and control of actions and projects themselves rather than the long-term outcomes of those actions and projects.

In addition, our attitude to market forces will also require some rethinking. For, while free markets are clearly creative self-organising systems, the new science tells us that the long-term futures of such systems are unknowable. It also tells us that there is nothing about the nature or operation of self-organising systems which either maximises or optimises outcomes. The forces of selection (competition) weed out all systems that are not flexible. There can be no *guarantee*, therefore, that competition and free markets will 'optimise' anything other than flexibility itself. It is no more possible to predict the precise outcome of market forces over the longer term than it is the outcome of a planned system. It is an advantage that free-market policies allow outcomes to evolve and do not require some prediction of the future. But the implication is that we cannot determine at the outset where a market economy will go. All of this is clear as soon as we face the possibility that the future of such systems may be unknowable.

Freedom of Choice and Constraints

The new science invites planners and free marketeers alike to reconsider that old conundrum – the relationship between freedom of choice and constraints. On the old view, successful organisations and economies were those which achieved a predictable equilibrium adaptation to their environments. Then members of such a system only had a choice in so far as environmental constraints were loose. The new science tells us that creative systems are far from equilibrium. They operate where they are *not* adapted to their environments and successful futures are therefore not constrained by those environments. The relevant system and its environment co-evolve in a manner determined by the interaction between them. Consequently, the members of a system have free choice of actions, but the price they pay is that they cannot know the long-term outcomes of those actions. Therefore, they cannot know whether the outcomes will prove desirable or not. The trade-off seems to be this: a firm or an economy can be made stable by constraining it with rules, regulations and plans and the result will be certain stagnation. The alternative is to free the firm or economy so that it relies on self-organising interaction, learning and market processes; then creativity becomes possible. But the specific outcome is unknowable.

Scientists have shown that, in nature, relationships are intricate because of complex feedback loops. For example, A affects B, which in turn affects A, which has a further effect on B, and so on. Thus, in the atmosphere, air pressure, precipitation and heat intermingle in producing the changing weather patterns across the seasons, year in and year out. The same is true of economies: economic agents interact and economic variables are interrelated. For instance, consumer spending affects income, which in turn affects consumer spending, as well as other macro-economic variables such as investment and employment, which themselves have an impact on consumption. These in turn affect income – and so on in a continuing series of complicated feedbacks.

Where feedbacks are 'negative', they dampen the system, leading to declining effects. Consequently, the system moves, in the absence of external shocks or what are sometimes called *stochastic effects**, to a stable point or stable equilibrium. Macro-economic relationships have usually been thought of in this way (for example, the national income multiplier eventually fizzles out). In other cases, a limit cycle can result. Movement occurs regularly between two points, from X to Y and then back to X unendingly. The textbook stable 'cobweb' model for hog prices is the classic example and sometimes the business cycle is represented in this way, though both in reality are far from being stable. Hog prices vary in a far more complex fashion; business cycles are rarely so predictable. What could explain such greater complexity? As we have already pointed out, real life results are frequently put down to 'noise' or effects external to the model.

But scientists can now demonstrate that complex behaviour is part of nature and that such behaviour does not rely on external shocks. In nature, feedbacks are positive as well as negative, leading to a magnification of small causes. So a

[17]

stable point or a limit cycle is not the only possible, or even necessarily the most likely, outcome. Economists have recognised the possibility of 'explosive instability' – the textbook cobweb model usually includes an example – but have normally passed over it quickly for the very good reason that markets and economies do not seem to explode. Chaos theory highlights how behaviour can be highly complex without being explosive.

Chaos, Management and Economics

Recent advances in science suggest that it is now time to think again about economic behaviour. Chaos theory, which relates to circumstances of tension between forces of stability and instability, questions many of the explicit and implicit assumptions of accepted economic analysis. It also raises fundamental questions about the way businesses are managed. Chaotic environments require a different style of management from environments where negative feedbacks lead to stability. The same is true of government policy-making. Throughout this *Hobart Paper*, for convenience, the terms 'management' and 'manager' are used but they should be understood to include policy-makers in government and government agencies.

Opponents of the application of chaos to the study of management and economies will raise the objection that few proven cases of chaos exist in the social sciences. Our answer to such an objection takes two forms. *First*, the idea that unless one can 'prove' statistically that something happens, it should be discounted is not one with which we are comfortable. To discover chaos statistically requires large amounts of 'unpolluted' data – that is, data unaffected by 'noise' or stochastic factors. Such data rarely if ever exist in economies. Moreover, traditional statistical methods are largely inappropriate for the discovery of chaos and the quantitative methods developed specifically for chaotic systems are relatively new and limited in scope (Brock, Hsieh and LeBaron, 1991).[1]

---

1 As Israel Kirzner (1976, p.47), an economist in the 'Austrian' tradition, notes: 'The real world includes a whole range of matters beyond the scope of the measuring instruments of the econometrician. Economic science must be able to encompass this realm.' The complementary nature of Austrian economics and chaos theory is discussed in Chapter IV (below, p.88).

We would turn the onus of proof around and argue that it is at least as incumbent on the doubters to demonstrate that chaos has no relevance to the study of management and economies as it is for others to show that it has. To put the point another way, doubters must explain why businesses and economies, with all their multitude of feedback loops, are exempt from the complex dynamics discovered in so many other areas of life. We take up this issue again in Chapter IV.

Secondly, long study of management and economics has led to a mountain of theories and econometric analysis. Nevertheless, commerce and economies continue to surprise. Somehow, away from the textbook and the classroom, there appears to be a hidden complexity in economic life which continuously pokes fun at established theory. The arrival of a mode of thought which challenges the whole way the world is viewed is timely, if only because the way it is now seen is so patently unable to explain events, except in the *ex post* sense. A new way of looking at economic relationships seems desirable since the existing dominant paradigm in economics (neo-classical economics) appears incapable of handling their complexity.

Undoubtedly, what has so far limited the spread of knowledge about chaos, both inside and outside the academic world, is the formidable mathematics in most books and articles on the subject. Precise expression of chaotic dynamics requires mathematics. But, since our objective in this *Hobart Paper* is to bring the message of chaos to the widest possible audience, we shun mathematical notation. Instead, we demonstrate the main arguments of the theory in words, analogies, pictures and diagrams (the only exception is a brief and simple mathematical appendix at the end of Chapter II which can be skipped). Scientists, mathematicians and econometricians already have a library of technical texts on chaos theory (see, for example, Berge, Pomeau and Vidal, 1984; Stewart, 1989; Wiggins, 1990; Medio, 1992; Granger and Terasvirta, 1992). Our objective is to show to businessmen, economists and a wider body of students, academics and policy-makers how chaos has profound implications for the way businesses and economies are viewed.

The *Paper* is organised as follows. Chapter II briefly charts the development of chaos theory and explains its main features. Chapter III examines the significance of chaos theory for management, including the way businesses are organised. The significance for economics and more especially economic policy is explored in Chapter IV. The concluding Chapter V emphasises the main lessons of chaos theory for managers and economic policy-makers. The overriding message is that the long-term strategies of businesses and economies cannot be successfully planned, although of course the short-term day-to-day activities of businesses and the execution of their projects can and must be. Instead of long-term planning, the aim should be to create the conditions most conducive to a *process* of continuous change.

II. THE MEANING OF CHAOS

'The simplest systems are now seen to create extraordinarily difficult problems of predictability.'   (James Gleick, 1988, pp.7-8)

Ever since people began to try making conscious sense of their lives, they have wanted to determine how much of what happens to them flows from their choices and how much is determined by factors beyond their individual and joint control. Theologians have long argued about the place of free will. Closer to home, economists and politicians have debated fiercely the extent to which government can determine the development of economies. Management practitioners and theorists continue to argue about the degree to which an organisation's success is determined by the choices of its managers. Beliefs about unresolved questions of choice and constraint, or free will as against determinism, are major influences on the kinds of actions that are prescribed and taken.

The discoveries made by scientists and mathematicians, in exploring the nature of complexity, shed new light on choices and constraints in social systems, including what is possible and what is impossible for managers and economic policy-makers. These important discoveries relate to the properties of non-linear feedback systems. The first step in understanding how modern scientific theories of complexity throw light on the nature of choice is therefore to grasp the concept of non-linear feedback in human organisations by considering how individuals interact.

The Complexity of Cause and Effect

Consider in the simplest and most general of terms the behaviour of three individuals, X, Y and Z, as depicted in Figure 1. Looking at the interactions between the three from the perspective of X, X operates within an environment which consists of the other two, in the following manner. X discovers by some means what Y and Z are doing, chooses how to respond appropriately and then acts. That action has consequences which Y and Z then discover. In turn this leads

Figure 1: Illustrating Feedback

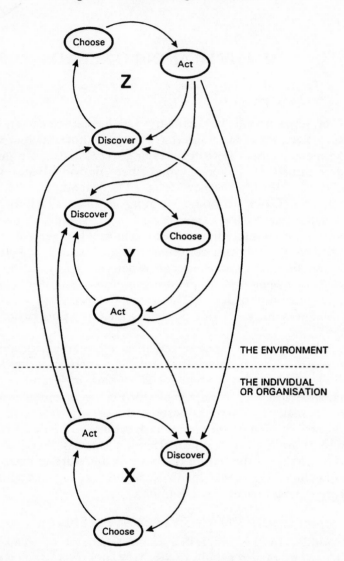

each of them to choose a response which, of course, has consequences that X then discovers and responds to, and so on. Thus every action X takes feeds back to have an impact on his or her next action. The same applies to Y and Z. Thus, in day-to-day life, as individuals interact, they constitute a feedback system.

Figure 1 can also be interpreted in terms of the behaviour of three groups of people or in terms of three organisations. The concept can be expanded to incorporate large numbers of organisations interacting in an economic or social environment. This includes coalitions of individuals, groups or companies. It follows that all human systems are feedback systems. Furthermore, those systems always involve non-linear relationships.

In a linear system there is one and only one effect for each cause. There is, therefore, essentially no choice of outcome. In linear systems, the combined effect of two different causes is merely the addition of the effect of each cause taken individually. This means that linear systems can be understood by analysing them into their component parts and studying each component. The whole is simply the sum of the parts. Linear systems lend themselves to being solved and hence to being 'engineered'.

By contrast, in non-linear systems one cause may have a variety of effects, thus making choice a real possibility. Also, a non-linear system may be much more than the sum of its parts, so it is impossible fully to understand the system simply by analysing it into its components. Such complex systems are far more difficult to engineer successfully since potential outcomes can be formidably difficult to identify, let alone measure. People have choices, they often react in ways that are stubbornly individual, even peculiar, and group behaviour is more than simply the sum of individual behaviours.

Non-Linear Behaviour

It is now well-recognised that people behave in a non-linear way. To take an example: Amos Tversky of Stanford University, in an influential psychological study of human behaviour, demonstrated that people can be risk-averse when expecting a gain and risk-seeking when facing a loss. Asked in an experiment whether they would prefer $85,000 or the *chance* of $100,000, most people said they would take the money. Asked then whether they would rather lose $85,000 or run an 85 per cent risk of losing $100,000, most people opted to take the chance. A linear system does not allow for such asymmetric effects.

Financial markets have also been associated with non-linearity, in the sense that the same-sized cause is quite capable of having different effects depending on the circumstances. For instance, the effect of a 1 per cent interest rate cut on the financial markets depends upon how the markets interpret it (*The Economist*, 9 October 1993, p.10). Recently it has been discovered that after large negative shocks, industrial production tends to return to positive growth more quickly than implied by traditional linear models (Terasvirta and Anderson, 1993).

Attempts by mathematicians and natural scientists to grapple with the complicated dynamics of non-linear feedback systems developed at first separately, in a number of different areas of study. Serious scientific study of the mathematics of such systems goes back to Henri Poincaré in the late 19th century, who was studying motions in the solar system. Poincaré demonstrated that simple systems of a non-linear kind can produce complicated and random-like behaviour. The importance of his work was little recognised at the time, however, and complementary studies in Russia and later in the USSR (for instance, Lyapunov, 1892; Kolmogorov, 1941) also remained little known to Western scientists.

The study of non-linear feedback systems came to life in the West in the 1960s, especially due to the work of Edward Lorenz (1963) on atmospheric turbulence and studies by Mitchell Feigenbaum (1978) on bifurcations and by Stephen Smale (1963 and 1980) and Ruelle and Takens (1971) on *fractal** dimensions and *attractors**. In the USA, Smale's study of the mathematics of non-linear dynamics demonstrated that following very small events, the time-path or trajectory of a system can become highly complex, leading to *chaotic turbulence**.

Chaotic turbulence has now become a key part of the study of thermodynamics, where it was developed to deal with a class of systems called *dissipative structures**, a term coined by Ilya Prigogine (1980). Non-linear electrical circuits, solar pulsations, measles epidemics, acoustic turbulence, some chemical reactions, and hydrodynamic turbulence have all been linked to chaotic dynamics. The complexity of fluid motion can, for example, be observed in the movement of water in a stream or river. Some water moves slowly and other parts move quickly. Some water spins around creating mini-whirlpools. Other parts may move in an opposite direction to the general flow. Turbulence is caused by viscosity or friction within the water which dissipates energy. Viscosity introduces non-linearity into the equations of motion, making turbulent outcomes possible.

It is now established in biology that complex oscillations in behaviour are widespread in life from the cell to the whole organism. This includes rhythms in respiration, cardiac muscle contraction and reproduction cycles in plants. Electrical activity of the brain in deep sleep has been found to act as a system with great intrinsic complexity and unpredictability. It has indeed been claimed by one of the leading pioneers of chaos theory that 'the dynamical complexity of the human brain cannot be an accident. It must have been selected for its very instability' (Prigogine, 1988, p.98). Similarly, Edward Lorenz's work on climate has shown why atmospheric conditions are inherently unpredictable − beyond a few days ahead, at best. Climate, like nature in general, is a highly complex mixture of instability within stability. The weather may be unpredictable more than a few days ahead, but it stays within bounds. We know London will not have a temperature of 90°F in January. We know it will not snow in Singapore. Non-linear feedback systems produce a mixture of order and disorder.

Positive versus Negative Feedbacks

Non-linear feedback systems are driven by positive and negative feedback. Domestic central heating systems, for example, are controlled in a negative feedback way. A desired temperature is set, then a sensor measures actual room temperature and compares it with the desired level. The deviation is then fed into the control system to turn the system on if the temperature is too low or to turn it off if the temperature is too high. Such feedback is negative in the sense that the action leads to consequences which offset or cancel out the original deviation.

Any planned system is based on the notion of negative feedback. Some intended outcome, or at least some intended direction of movement, is deliberately set. Then outcomes are monitored and the gap between actual and intended is identified. Next, action is taken to narrow the gap by feeding modifications back into the system so as to secure the convergence of actual and intended. Keynesian demand management is essentially of this kind. Fiscal policy is intended to smooth out fluctuations in the economy by affecting aggregate demand, in a similar way to that by which the central heating system adjusts room temperature.

As explained in Chapter I, positive feedback is the opposite of negative feedback. Instead of feeding back the discrepancy between an outcome and an intention in a manner that closes a gap between the two, the feedback *progressively widens* the gap. Thus, if positive feedback prevailed in the case of a domestic central heating system, when actual temperature exceeded the desired level, the deviation would be fed into the control system. This would then cause *more* heat to be pumped into the room causing the actual temperature to rise even further above that desired. *Positive feedback does not cancel out deviations, rather it reinforces them.* Therefore, while negative feedback is dampening and stabilising, positive feedback is amplifying and destabilising. In an economy, it is now recognised that misapplied or naïve demand management policies can have similar effects. The result is increased, not reduced, economic instability (Dow, 1970).

Positive feedback appears to be widespread in economic and business life. It can take the form of self-reinforcing growth, bandwagon effects, chain reactions, self-fulfilling prophecies, and virtuous and vicious circles. Furthermore, negative and positive feedback can be seen as two different types of learning in organisations. Figure 2 depicts managers and policy-makers going around a rational feedback loop at the centre of the diagram. They do so in a manner in which both their discoveries about how the world operates, and the manner in which they choose and act, are governed by a shared mental model or paradigm. Because they do not question that model they are practising what Argyris and Schön (1978) called 'single-loop learning'. They are learning about the consequences of their behaviour and adjusting their behaviour in the light of that learning. But they are not questioning the frame of reference within which their learning takes place. Single-loop learning is a negative feedback process associated with stabilising behaviour.

As the level of uncertainty and ambiguity rises, however, it becomes ineffective and dangerous to operate according to a mental model formulated and shared in conditions that have now changed dramatically. What is therefore required is a *double-loop learning* in which the shared mental model is

[26]

Figure 2: Single-Loop Learning

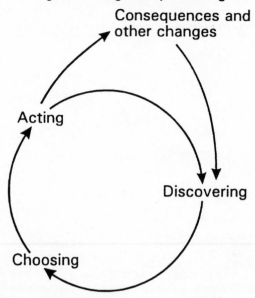

questioned and changed (Figure 3). Double-loop learning is a positive feedback process of attending to the contradictions and conflicts between what is actually happening and the expectations to which an outdated mental model leads. Thus a new mental model is acquired, which becomes the previous mental model as far as the next discovery is concerned. Double-loop learning therefore has a destructive aspect. It is a process of making old perceptions redundant. But it also has a creative aspect in that it leads to a new mental model or paradigm. Double-loop learning has been an essential component of human development from the earliest times. It is essentially destabilising because it challenges the *status quo*.

Chaotic Systems and Bounded Instability

Planning and similar forms of control, at both the micro- (organisational) and macro-economic levels, are essentially driven by negative feedback. They are intended to produce *predictable* patterns of behaviour. This then facilitates optimal adaptation of the organisation, market or entire economy to a *given* or known environment. In a negative feedback system there are identifiable conditions, or parameter values, within that system which cause it to settle down. It is attracted to a

Figure 3: Double-Loop Learning

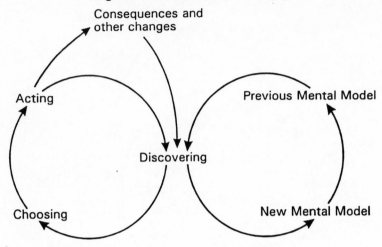

point from which it will move only if there is an external 'shock'. This amounts to attraction to a state of stable equilibrium – a state in which the system does not change or changes only in repetitive and therefore predictable ways. The equilibrium of neo-classical economics is of this type. Such systems may be efficient, in the sense that repetition helps them to do better and better what they already do well. But, by the same token, they cannot do anything innovative or new: they are not creative. Neo-classical economics has a problem introducing novelty and innovation, a point to which we return later.

Equilibrium behaviour is an either/or choice. Either the system is driven by negative feedback and tends to stable equilibrium or it is driven by positive feedback and tends to uncontrollable instability. If that instability is to be removed, then some agent or condition outside the system has to 'step in and put a stop to it'. Non-linear feedback systems are not, however, confined to 'either/or' behaviour. This produces the paradox of stability within instability. When systems are far from equilibrium, they automatically apply *internal* constraints to keep instability within boundaries. This is so because of the non-linear structure of the system.

Positive feedback processes amplify and spread disturbances. In the extreme, they could make an organisation, market or economy explosively unstable. From a linear view of the world the instability would be unending. The trajectory would shoot upwards (or downwards) unless disturbed by external intervention. But non-linear systems of a chaotic nature can be highly complex and seemingly unstable. Yet they remain constrained because of the existence of what scientists call a *strange attractor**.

Normal, Periodic and 'Strange' Attractors

A normal attractor is the equilibrium or limit time-path of a system. Imagine a ball placed inside a fruit bowl. Shake the bowl and the ball shoots up one side and then back across or around the sides to the other and then back again to the first side. But it eventually settles down to the bottom of the bowl. It is attracted to a stable equilibrium point or what is a fixed-point attractor. A point attractor is a steady state – the system does not evolve or change. The ball always ends up in the bottom of the bowl. The outcome is fully predictable.

By contrast, a clock pendulum is a classic case of a regular, periodic motion which constantly repeats itself (the limit cycle). In this case the system is said to have a periodic attractor. The pendulum swings regularly back and forth, from one point to another, hour after hour. Where behaviour is neither stable nor cyclical but chaotic, however, it is far more complex than in either of these cases. The movement in the system is determined by a 'strange attractor'. Unlike the other two attractors, a strange attractor is associated with complex oscillations (hence its name). It is a set of points, rather than one point, to which movements starting off in the neighbourhood are drawn. The path is aperiodic and never reaches a stable equilibrium. Equally, it does not follow a regular cycle like a pendulum. At the same time it has bounded movement and is not completely unstable. The motions are contained within the region of the attractor.

For any non-linear feedback system there can be points within it to which the system is drawn that do not produce a stable equilibrium point or a regular (periodic) cycle. Instead, the product is far more complex behaviour. The system becomes a mixture of stability and instability. Think of the ball in the fruit bowl moving about within the bowl in what appears to be a random fashion. It is never, however, allowed to leave the bowl and therefore its movement is bounded. Because of the complexity of the movements, for all practical purposes the system can *seem* completely unstable and unpredictable.

Complex behaviour, associated with a strange attractor, is to be found at the borders between stability and instability. If a non-linear feedback system is driven from the stable state, it passes through a *phase transition** – one of the most important discoveries of recent science.

The Mandelbrot Set

One way of understanding the nature of this discovery is to take a very simple non-linear system, one that generates a sequence of numbers. Starting from a given set of numbers, a computer can calculate the sequence generated by a feed-back loop, and can show whether the result is a stable pattern, such as a straight line. It can also show whether the result is a regular cycle or irregular and unstable movement. The computer can plot a map showing all those sets of starting numbers which lead to stability against a background of all the sets of numbers which lead to instability.

A commonly used example is the feedback equation that generates what is called the 'Mandelbrot set', named after its discoverer, Benoit Mandelbrot (for further information see Mandelbrot, 1977; Gleick, 1988; Stewart, 1989). Mandelbrot was researching the nature of mathematical shapes which did not fit traditional Euclidean concepts of form. That is to say, he was looking at irregularities of shapes and forms, such as ferns, broccoli, clouds, mountains and coastlines, rather than regular shapes such as triangles and rectangles. A computer drawing up the conditions leading to instability using the equation $Z_t = Z^2_{t-1} + c$, where t indicates each loop and c is a complex number, produces the pattern shown in Figure 4.[1]

First impressions may suggest there is nothing at all surprising about this map. There is a large black blob in the middle which represents all combinations of starting events that yield stable outcomes (attraction to a stable point or a regular cycle – that is, equilibrium). Outside this blob, there

---

1 A complex number is one that is written in two parts to address its point east and north in a complex plane. The pattern is generated by starting from where Z is zero. Multiply Z by itself and add the complex number, c. Then take the result and multiply it by itself and again add c. This process is repeated a large number of times.

Figure 4: Stability and Instability

Source: Penrose (1989)

is a large white area for all events that lead to instability. The surprise comes, however, when the border between stability and instability is closely studied. The border is not clean-cut, nor a clear line dividing the two regions. Instead, it represents a completely different form of behaviour – one that until recently very few scientists knew anything about. The discovery demonstrates that in non-linear feedback systems we are not confronted by a simple choice between stability and instability. They can operate in a third state, that of *bounded instability**, which is qualitatively different from either stability or instability.

More light can be shed on this phenomenon by taking smaller and smaller intervals between the sets of starting numbers at the border line. The product (Figure 5) is a border that consists of complex, highly irregular wispy lines.

When one of these wispy lines is examined in more detail, the computer draws a complex pattern of the kind shown in Figure 6. The patterns in Figure 6 are drawn in black and white, but the computer could be instructed to use different

Figure 5: Illustrating the Complex Border Region

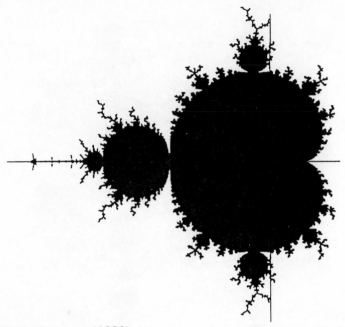

Source: Penrose (1989)

colours according to how long it takes to identify whether an initial set of numbers will end up as an unstable sequence. With these instructions, the computer will draw a contour map of the strength of the pull to instability. The result is patterns of great beauty (see, for example, Peitgen and Richter, 1986; Gleick, 1988).

Part of the pattern in Figure 6 can be blown up and other patterns embedded in it exposed. What is seen depends each time on how closely the map is examined. It is always different and yet always similar. Recognisable if irregular patterns always appear.

Tiny differences in perspective, tiny differences between the initial sets of numbers, lead to different yet recognisably similar patterns to the original shape. Islands of stability pop up over and over again. These patterns can be said to be constant only in the degree of their irregularity.

This form of behaviour is not limited to numbers and computer simulations. What intrigues scientists is that it is repeated time and again in nature – for example, the weather

Figure 6: Order within Disorder

system displays just such behaviour, as do turbulent liquids and gases. Tucked away between stability and instability, at the frontier, non-linear feedback systems generate forms of behaviour that are neither stable nor unstable. They are continuously new and creative. This property applies to non-linear feedback systems no matter where they are found.

There is an infinitely intricate border region that is, in effect, an intertwining of order and disorder. At the border the variety of forms generated is such that the system is one of continuous creation.

Stretching and Folding Behaviour – 'Fractal' or Chaotic

In this border area it is impossible to make clear-cut distinctions between stability and instability because the starting conditions that lead to the one are so close to the starting conditions that lead to the other. So close are they that it is not possible to measure or act upon the differences between them. *It is not possible to determine in advance which end-condition is going to occur.* The specific future of the system is effectively unknowable. Nonetheless, such behaviour has an overall, 'hidden', qualitative pattern. Mandelbrot coined the term 'fractal' to refer to the shapes he found. A fractal is a geometric shape in which similar patterns are repeated at several different scales. The shapes are similar no matter how closely they are examined. We can get a feel for what is involved if we think of a system that 'stretches and folds like a baker's dough' (Kamminga, 1990, p.56). Instead of exploding exponentially, the system turns back on itself in a process of 'folding', which merges widely separated points and keeps them bounded. The result is behaviour which is fractal or chaotic. It is exactly this combination of stretching and folding that leads to chaos (Medio, 1992, p.121).

These conclusions about chaotic behaviour flow from the non-linear structure of the system itself. They are not the result of the nature of the environment in which the system operates. Far from equilibrium, behaviour is both stable and unstable, and not because some agent within it or outside it intervenes (say, applies random shocks to the system). It results because the non-linear structure of the feedback loop causes it to happen. Fairly constant cycles of behaviour can occur, interrupted from time to time and without warning by phases of chaotic turbulence. Such qualitative changes in behaviour need not result, as is often assumed (notably in economics), from exogenous (external) effects or 'stochastic noise'. The aperiodic motion is not due to a change in the underlying relationship or structure of the system. Nor is it due to stochastic or random disturbances. *It is pre-determined within the system.*

[34]

In the border region between stability and instability, the behaviour of the system unfolds in a complex manner. The product is so dependent upon the detail of what happens that the links between cause and effect are lost. It is no longer possible to count on a certain input leading to a certain output. The laws of the system operate to escalate small chance disturbances along the way, breaking the link between an input and a subsequent output.

Sensitive Dependence

Such ideas lead to the property of sensitive dependence on initial conditions. Sensitive dependence is an important feature of the disorderly behaviour of deterministic dynamic systems in science. In particular, it is responsible for their unpredictability, for the system can be sensitive to even minute changes in the value of its conditions or parameters. Very small variations in parameter values lead to huge variations in behaviour of the system (Schuster, 1989, p.63). The system can go from periodic to chaotic and back again even though the parameter values are very close together (see the appendix to this chapter, below, pp.42-46).

In chaotic behaviour, a system operates to amplify tiny changes in conditions into major alterations of consequent behaviour. This is what lies behind the 'butterfly effect', first observed by Edward Lorenz, who was attempting to predict weather patterns. The sensitivity may be so great that differences in the value of a condition or parameter to a number of decimal points could eventually alter the behaviour of the system completely. Tiny changes that could not possibly be detected could lead the system to totally different states of behaviour. Sensitive dependence has important implications for the study of management and economics. In practice, when assessing real systems, such as economic systems, initial conditions can rarely if ever be precisely specified. Measurement errors and 'noise' will usually be present. Also, it can never be safely presumed that all of the factors that may have an effect on behaviour are included in the model.

Self-Organisation

When non-linear feedback systems are pushed far from equilibrium into chaos, they are capable of spontaneously

[35]

producing unpredictable, more complex forms of behaviour through a process of self-organisation. Fractals are evidence of self-organising systems. Fractal shapes are self-similar, that is to say, they have similar structures on all scales and they are now known to be common in nature. A snowflake is a good example, as is a tree leaf; watching the clouds reveals further evidence of natural self-organising and complex patterns. In other words, in non-linear feedback systems in nature, continuously creative and innovative behaviour *emerges*. At the boundary between stability and instability, the system produces an endless stream of new and creative forms. Experimenters seeking to influence the outcome would have to operate on the boundary conditions – that is, they would have to operate upon the context or situation within which the behaviour is occurring. They cannot determine what the system will do in specific terms; all they can do is bring about some general pattern of behaviour if the right environmental conditions are created.

In the old Newtonian mind-set of the scientist, nature's systems were thought to behave in predictable or predetermined ways. To discover them simply meant more research. The bounty would be full knowledge of the system, resulting in an ability to control and plan successfully. The same mind-set applied (and still does) in much social science research. If we can find out what causes poverty or leads to inflation or causes juvenile crime or determines unemployment, then society can be organised to end poverty, inflation, juvenile crime and unemployment. It is recognised that problems could arise if there are conflicts in the required policies. For example, lower inflation might lead to higher unemployment, at least for some time. But essentially this is posed as a question of choice, usually political choice. It is not allowed to disrupt the view that the system can be planned.

From a chaos perspective, however, the planning of specific long-term outcomes is bound to lead to disappointment. Chaotic systems are driven by complex feedback processes. Hence, links between precise cause and effect are usually impossible to identify; we cannot therefore act on such links. Instead, order may emerge unpredictably from chaos without formal design, although there is no guarantee that it will.

Dissipative Structures

Evidence of the importance of 'emergence' as a fundamental property of non-linear feedback systems comes from Ilya Prigogine's work on what are called dissipative systems (Prigogine and Stengers, 1984). Dissipative systems contain forces due to friction that dissipate energy, but they still preserve a structure. An example will help to clarify the point.

A liquid is at a thermodynamic equilibrium when it is closed to its environment and its temperature is uniform throughout. Then the liquid is in a state of rest at a global level. That is, there are no bulk movements in it, although the molecules move everywhere and face in different directions. In equilibrium, then, the positions and movements of the molecules are random and hence independent of each other. At equilibrium nothing happens. The behaviour of the system is symmetrical, uniform and regular. Every point within the liquid is essentially the same as every other point. At every point in time the liquid is in exactly the same state as it is at every other.

When the liquid is pushed far from equilibrium by using some 'control parameter', say, an environmental condition such as heat, then the system uses positive feedback. This amplifies small fluctuations throughout the liquid. So, if at the start a layer of liquid is close to thermodynamic equilibrium and heat is applied to the base, that starts a fluctuation or change in the environmental condition in which the liquid exists. That temperature change is then amplified or spread throughout the liquid. The effect of this amplification is to break the symmetry and to cause differentiation within the liquid. At first the molecules at the base stop moving randomly and begin to move upward. Those most affected by the increase in temperature rise to the top.

That movement eventually starts convection so that those molecules least affected are displaced and pushed down to the base of the liquid. There they are heated and move up, in turn pushing others down. The molecules are now moving in a circle. The symmetry of the liquid is broken because of the bulk movement that has been set up. Now each point in the liquid is no longer the same. At some points movement is up and at others it is down. After a time, a critical temperature point is reached and a new structure emerges in the liquid. Molecules move in a regular direction, setting up hexagonal cells, some turning clockwise and others turning anti-clockwise. In other words, they *self-organise*. What this represents is *long-range coherence**. Molecular movements are now correlated with each other as if they were communicating. The direction of each cell's movement is, however, unpredictable. It cannot be determined in advance.

What direction any one cell takes depends upon small differences in the conditions that existed as the cell was formed. As further heat is applied to the liquid, the symmetry of the cellular pattern is broken and other patterns emerge. Eventually the liquid will reach a turbulent state of chaos. Movement from a perfectly orderly state to one of more complex order has occurred through a destabilising process. The system has been pushed away from a stable equilibrium towards chaos. The process is clearly one of destruction making way for creation of the new, in much the same sense as Joseph Schumpeter (1942) described 'gales of creative destruction' in economies.

The Properties of Dissipative Systems

Ilya Prigogine established that non-linear systems are changeable only when they are pushed far from an initial equilibrium, as in the case of liquid subject to heating. Non-linear systems can import energy or information from the environment which is then dissipated through the system, in a sense causing it to fall apart. But the system still has a structure (Prigogine's 'dissipative structure') in the form of irregular patterns capable of renewal through self-organisation. Dissipative systems have the following properties:

o They use positive feedback to amplify fluctuations in their environment so as to disrupt existing patterns of behaviour. The result, eventually, is irregular or fractal or chaotic patterns of behaviour. So there is great individual variety within a structure.

o There is structure as well as variety. The structure takes the form of correlations or communication between individual components of the system. This is self-organisation in much the same sense as F.A. Hayek (1948) used the term in his explanation of how societies change.

[38]

O They make choices at critical points. A system may have qualitatively different behaviour due to a small change in the control parameters (like turning up the heat slightly). The system suddenly flips from one type of behaviour to another. The old idea that small changes have small effects is no longer universally valid. Dissipative systems have multiple choices and the consequences of making one choice rather than another may be large and unpredictable.

O They evolve sometimes in unexpected and sudden ways, becoming increasingly complex. Time and space matter. The system's history is important and *new order emerges without prior intention.* Emergence means that outcomes are a surprise. For example, there is nothing in the nature of a stable liquid to indicate how it will perform under intense heat. Similarly in the financial markets, tens of thousands of man-hours of effort and millions of po unds have been spent on both computer systems and the analysts who feed them. Yet no one has found a way of reliably predicting movements in stock prices and foreign exchange rates. Similar efforts go into attempting to improve the forecasting of economies over the longer term (in terms of inflation, employment and economic growth rates, for example). Again, there is no evidence of sustained success.

Lessons from Chaos

Social organisations which are non-linear and have the capacity to behave as dissipative structures exhibit fractal-like qualities (Zimmerman and Hurst, 1992; Tsoukas, 1991; Stacey, 1991). Since human systems, including business organisations and economies, are non-linear feedback systems, the lessons from chaos are profound. Our contention is that business organisations and economies are essentially dissipative structures exhibiting both stability and instability *at the same time.* The spontaneous self-organisation of economic agents leads to unpredictable and emergent outcomes. Clearly, the implications of all this are dramatic for they rule out any notion of useful long-term planning, in the sense of

[39]

achieving specific, predicted outcomes. Instead, they make the case for establishing structures and processes that promote maximum adaptability.

Economic systems, in order to be changeable, must operate far from equilibrium where it is impossible for anyone to predict reliably the long-term outcomes. Consequently, no one can be in control of an economy. To be in control it would be necessary to have detailed knowledge of the complicated mathematical relationships of the system. There seems, however, to be no way such knowledge can be gleaned (Medio, 1992, p.85). Furthermore, because of the presence of *sensitive dependence on initial conditions** it would be necessary to measure all change with infinite accuracy. Clearly this is impossible.

The long-term future is not simply difficult to see, it is inherently unknowable because of the nature of the system itself and not because of changes going on outside it and having impacts on it. Such random factors add even more complexity. Consequently, decision-making processes that require reliable forecasts – even those based upon making assumptions about long-term future states – are called into question. Those applying such processes in conditions of bounded instability are engaging in fantasy.

There is no fundamental problem, at least in principle, in controlling the movement of a system to a fixed point in the future provided that it is an equilibrium system. To control movement to a future, distant point when the system is boundedly unstable is far more problematic. It would be essential to specify with complete accuracy each event and each action required to reach that future state. If there was a tiny error in specification, the system could amplify it, leading to a far different outcome from that planned.

In other words, it is not simply a matter of discovering the actions required to take a business or economy from one point to another. It is impossible to measure or record in such infinitely accurate detail for this to happen. Nor could some distant point be fixed upon and necessarily reached by trial and error because the errors would not cancel out. Some desirable end-state, a utopia, can be imagined and aimed for, but there is an infinitely small chance that it will ever actually be achieved. Unsurprisingly, world history is replete with failed attempts to create such utopias.

[40]

Making assumptions about the future state is also rather pointless because the assumptions would have to keep changing. It is not possible to envisage the precise future, let alone plan it in detail. The future of a chaotic system is open-ended and inherently unknowable. The system moves in a seemingly random way over the longer term, though it is in fact deterministic. The future emerges through spontaneous self-organisation. It is not possible to establish how the system will necessarily move before a policy change is made. *There is no alternative but to make the change and see what happens* – to discover where it is going as it is getting there.

The short-term future of chaotic systems is, however, more predictable because it takes time for the system to amplify tiny changes into important changes in patterns of behaviour. It is therefore perfectly possible, indeed essential, for people to design and plan their *next* actions. As explained in Chapter I, we have no argument with the notion of planning sequences of actions. It is the long-term outcomes of these actions that cannot be predicted in any useful sense. Instead, people have to learn as they go along and from that learning decide their next actions. Thus the future emerges.

The problem is not just the difficulty of forecasting the longer-term future accurately, given current knowledge or technology. Increasing the sophistication of forecasting methods and ever greater computer power are not the answers. In a chaotic system, no matter how much information about a system we have collected in the past, and no matter how much number crunching of the data occurs, the specific future cannot be predicted. A chaotic system is prone to sudden and unheralded qualitative changes, which may sometimes be of a dramatic nature. Clearly, chaos is more than simply a mathematical or scientific curiosity (Loye and Eisler, 1987; Cartwright, 1991). A common feature of its application is that it reveals the essentially unknowable future of creative systems.

APPENDIX: A Mathematical Note

We have so far shunned the use of mathematics. But the way in which a system becomes chaotic can be more precisely explained with the aid of a little mathematics. Readers can, of course, omit this appendix if they so wish.

A dynamic system can be represented as a set of equations relating the rate of change of each of the variables to some combination of the other variables (Frank and Stengos, 1988a, p.103; the following discussion draws heavily on this paper). This is not to say, of course, that the equations can necessarily be discovered.

It is now well understood in mathematical circles that systems of differential equations and systems of non-linear difference equations can generate very complex time-paths with motions that can appear random. Non-linear differential or difference equations can generate both cyclical and aperiodic motions. These motions may seem to be random but are, in fact, deterministic but chaotic.

One common mathematical example used to illustrate the fundamentals of chaos is a simple non-linear difference equation known as the 'logistic map', first used to model population dynamics in a pioneering investigation by the American biologist, Robert May. The equation takes the form:

$$X_t = a\, X_{t-1}\, (1 - X_{t-1}).$$

In this equation, which is quadratic and hence non-linear, the value of the parameter 'a' is crucial to the way the feedback system behaves. Quadratic behaviour is the simplest form of non-linearity. Also, the equation has a fixed time-lag. In practice, time-lags (reaction times) may not be constant in economic and business relationships and this adds further complexity and possible scope for chaotic outcomes (Invernizzi and Medio, 1991).

The equation has two fixed points or stationary solutions, $X_t = 0$ and $X_t = 1 - (1/a)$, producing a hill-shaped curve known as a 'phase curve'. Multiple fixed points are what cause non-

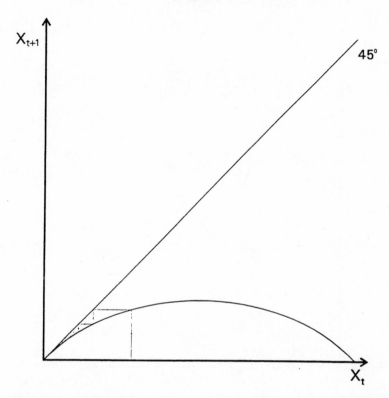

Figure 7: The Logistic Map: Stability at Zero
$0 < a < 1$

linear equations to have important properties for the discussion of chaos.

If initially the parameter 'a' is less than 1 but greater than 0, then the system tends to zero. So, if we are concerned with the impact of an increase in investment on economic growth, the impact would die out. This is shown in Figure 7.

Now suppose that 'a' is set between 1 and 3. Once 'a' is above 1, the phase curve will start above the 45-degree line and then intersect it. Figure 8 shows the more complex (and interesting) result. Suppose the starting point is X_1, then go vertically up to the function curve and proceed horizontally to the 45-degree line. This line shows where $X_t = X_{t+1}$, so it can be used to show the next stage of movement. Now proceed vertically from the 45-degree line to the function curve and then horizontally to the 45-degree line again.

Figure 8: The Logistic Map: Stability at other than Zero
$1 < a < 3$

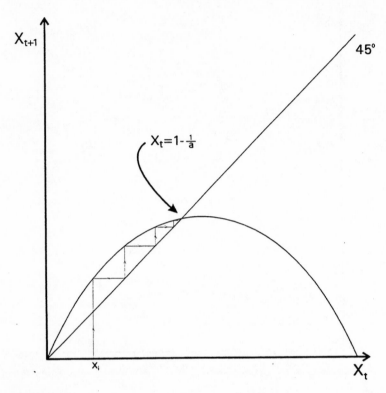

Continue to repeat these movements and in doing so the (simple) dynamics of the system are identified.

What is clear is that the system will move away from the fixed point, $X_t = 0$; and it will be attracted to the fixed point $X_t = 1-(1/a)$. $X_t = 1-(1/a)$ is therefore known as an 'attractor' (just as zero is the attractor in Figure 7).

Over a certain range of intervals of the parameter, what is quite unexpected is that this simple representation of a dynamic system can display chaotic behaviour. To see this, suppose that the parameter 'a' is gradually increased in size beyond 3. An extraordinary change takes place. The fixed point at $1-(1/a)$ becomes unstable. At $a = 3.2$ the system will have a 2-period (limit) cycle, which is stable. That is to say, the result is an oscillation between two points, like a clock pendulum. If 'a' is increased a little more, however, the

[44]

Figure 9: The Logistic Map: Chaos
e.g. $a \approx 3.8$

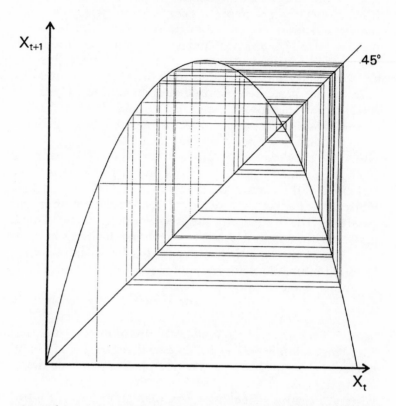

system becomes unstable. The result is at first a 4-stage cycle, then an 8-stage cycle, a 16-stage cycle, and so on. An important property of this sequence of period doublings, owed to Mitchell Feigenbaum, is that as 'a' increases, the range of values at which the parameter is associated with a particular stable cycle decreases. The result is a rapid growth of cycles. Once 'a' is greater than approximately 3.57 and less than 4, chaos occurs. The product is an infinite number of cycles with differing periodicity and an infinite number of fixed points (illustrated in Figure 9). The time-paths never repeat each other and we can say that chaos exists. The results and the actual time-path of the system depend crucially on the parameter value, in this case 'a', and the precise starting point.

Such behaviour depends on the shape of the function at its peak or the steepness of the 'hill' mapped out on the graph. It has been shown to apply in many areas of science and for similar and more complex functional forms. Equally, while the sequence of period doublings is one route to chaos, it is not the only route (though a common factor is typically some kind of *bifurcation* or splitting in two). From a bifurcation point two or more solution branches emerge which may be stable or unstable (Berge, Pomeau and Vidal, 1984, p.38).

Bifurcation theory began with pioneering work by Henri Poincaré and describes a sudden qualitative change in the system's behaviour or a 'phase transition'. This happens when a parameter is changed. In the logistics map, slow variations of the control parameter cause bifurcations. When bifurcations happen there is a discontinuous alteration in the nature of the system. In the above example, as 'a' was increased from 3 to 4 there was a period-doubling bifurcation. This is alternatively known as a 'flip bifurcation'. Other types of bifurcation, for example quasi-periodic or of an intermittent nature, are also possible.

Near a bifurcation point, the system is very sensitive to small fluctuations in its parameters and to external disturbances. Such changes influence the evolutionary path that the system will follow. The system may therefore be said to be *boundedly stable* in this phase. Where positive feedback dominates, vigorous and unstable growth in the system occurs. Where negative feedback predominates over positive feedback, the system remains dynamically stable until another bifurcation occurs.

In the above equation the degree of complexity was limited. There was only one dependent variable (X_t) and the system was described by what is technically called a first order difference equation. Systems represented by 'n' number of interdependent variables are said to have 'n dimensions', where 'n' is any number. Real life systems can be of this far more complex kind involving multiple dimensions and for which there may be no known mathematical solution. Indeed, a general mathematical theory exists only for one-dimensional, dynamic systems.

III. DISCOVERY, CHOICE AND ACTION IN ORGANISATIONS

'If choice is real, the future cannot be certain; if the future is certain, there can be no choice.' (Brian J. Loasby, 1976, p.5)

For some years the managers of General Motors have been formulating and implementing strategic plans with the explicit objective of recapturing their lost market share. Contrary to their intentions and expectations, however, the decline of General Motors has continued. Also, contrary to the intent of IBM's managers, and despite reorganisations and revitalisation programmes, it too is losing market share.

These are just two well-known examples of an apparently more widespread management inability to:

O design 'changeable organisations' – that is, organisations capable of continuing variety and innovation; and

O realise the outcomes they intend when their organisations do change (Beer, Eisenstat and Spector, 1990).[1]

'Lack of Changeability' Leads to Crisis in Organisations

The lack of changeability in organisations has been ascribed to cognitive factors. Managers behave according to a shared 'company recipe', which leads them to screen out suggested changes until the need for change reaches crisis proportions. Major strategic redirection then follows the years of strategic drift (Fine, 1984; Meyerson and Martin, 1987; Johnson, 1987). To put this another way, a failure of understanding on the part of an organisation's managers leads the organisation to drift away from a 'fit' with its competitive environment until some crisis provokes a return to equilibrium.

According to another but similar explanation, organisational inertia (personal commitments, financial investments

---

1 Part of this chapter draws from Ralph Stacey (1993), *Strategic Management and Organisational Dynamics*, London: Pitman. We would like to thank Pitman for permission to reproduce Figures 10-14 below which are from that book.

and institutional mechanisms supporting the *status quo*) prevents change. This goes on until accumulated stress, arising from a mismatch between existing strategy and environmental change, provokes a renewal of strategy. At this time the organisation is re-matched to its environment (Johnson, 1988; Miller and Friesen, 1980). According to this approach, the problem with corporations such as General Motors and IBM is failure by management to plan their businesses to change in some optimal sense to meet future market conditions.

This view flows quite logically from the management literature which is dominated by models of managerial behaviour in which the long-term outcomes of management actions are generally assumed to be predictable. They are therefore capable of intentional realisation. Each realisation is assumed to be an adaptation to the environment. The dynamic systems literature (Forrester, 1958 and 1961; Senge, 1990) does recognise that connections between cause and effect can be distant in place and time, making it likely that unintended and unexpected behaviour patterns will emerge. But it is still held that if only managers would operate at 'leverage points', where some small actions could lead to major outcomes, they would be able to move their businesses in the desired direction. Success is widely equated with planning for an *adaptive fit*** with the environment. In short, success is equated with management staying in control and realising long-term intentions.[2]

---

2 For example, Peter Senge (1990) emphasises the need for 'vision' and 'purpose'. While accepting that the world is complex with numerous and ill-recognised feedback effects, he still hankers for a world in which a clear sense of direction is appropriate. Similarly, Tom Peters (1987) and Michael Porter (1990) acknowledge the complexity of modern business life and hence the need for relentless change and adaptability. Peters uses the term 'chaos', though he seems to be using it in the everyday sense of muddle and confusion. Nevertheless, both still appear to believe that there is some kind of 'checklist' of fairly precise attributes that companies should adopt (or in Porter's study, nations should adopt). Adopting these attributes will in some sense guarantee competitive advantage. The same is only to a slightly lesser extent true of John Kay's (1993) recent pronouncements on how to achieve corporate success by having 'distinctive capabilities'. The 'capabilities' are widely defined and the need for flexibility is emphasised, which is something we endorse. In our view, however, it is not clear that the actual capabilities that have served some large firms well in the past will necessarily be the appropriate ones for the future, as Kay seems to imply.

The study of systems from a chaos perspective suggests a quite different view of management (although for convenience we use the term 'management', the arguments apply equally to policy-makers and administrators within government). This different view is based on the argument that organisations are changeable only when they are sustained far from an equilibrium fit with their environment and consequently are unstable in a certain sense (Stacey, 1991 and 1992; Zimmerman, 1992). The links between actions and long-term outcome are so unpredictable that it is inherently impossible for managers to design and realise *intended* long-term outcomes. Today's dominant understanding of the reasons for organisational failure is therefore reversed. Organisations stumble, not because they fail to plan to achieve a 'fit' with their future environments (achieving 'adaptive fit'), but because *they simply adapt instead of create*, and they do not realise long-term intended outcomes because *it is impossible to do so*. General Motors and IBM can adapt to the immediate past, and to present conditions. They cannot change now for future conditions, however, because they *cannot know* the competitive environment they will then face.

In our view, the failure of managements to realise their intended long-term plans lies in the irremovable properties of organisational systems rather than in some form of management incompetence. Only when a system operates in a chaotic or fractal state is it capable of endless and surprising variety. In other words, natural selection weeds out all systems that reach states of either complete instability or complete stability. The survivors or thrivers are systems that are sustained far from equilibrium, in bounded instability. In the paradoxical state known as chaos they are inherently changeable, thus capable of continuing innovation and variety.

The 'Rational' Model of Management

A process of decision-making and control is simply a particular way of discovering, choosing and acting. When managers make decisions and carry out control procedures, when advisers recommend methods of making decisions and practising control, they are all, in effect, using some particular process model, which is generally used without questioning the model's assumptions about the nature of feedback. Feedback may be either negative or positive. The kind of process model constructed will depend on which of these kinds of feedback is emphasised (Hanna, 1988).

In the planning approach to organisational management, which in the past has dominated the management literature, discovery is the systematic collection of objectively factual, often quantitative, data. This is then carefully analysed to generate options for managerial evaluation and choice. In turn, choice is a process of setting objectives and evaluating the identified options using general criteria such as acceptability, feasibility and 'adaptive fit' with the environment. The option then selected is the one most likely to achieve the objective. In this process, action is defined as the implementation of the selected option. What happens to an organisation is assumed to be determined primarily by the shared intention or the joint choices about long-term outcome of its managers, as embodied in their plans, and those choices are the result of a 'rational' decision-making process. Industrial organisation forms of strategy formulation (for example, Thompson, 1967; Williamson, 1975; Porter, 1980 and 1985) are of this type. They suggest a necessity for organisations to scan their external environment to maintain a kind of organisational equilibrium or 'adaptive fit'.

As they implement their chosen plans, in practice managers move around a discovery, choice and action loop. In doing so, they encounter the constraints their environment places upon them, which mean that outcomes differ from those expected. This is dealt with in the planning model by comparing actual outcomes with planned outcomes. Variances are calculated and choices are made among options to remove any variance. Corrective action is then taken to restore the organisation to the planned path (as in the example of the central heating system discussed in Chapter II, above, p.25). Constraints on managerial choice are thus dealt with by the use of monitoring forms of control, intended to enable an organisation to continue along the long-term path chosen by its managers. The result is a form of stability and regularity.

But there is a problem in understanding what 'choice' means when success requires adaptation to a given or known environment. The environment must determine what the

Figure 10: The Rational Approach to Management

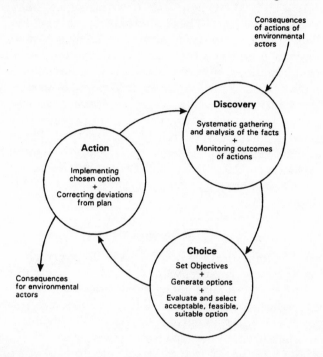

successful state will be. In this world, managerial decision-making becomes simply a calculation to determine what the successful adaptation is, leaving no room for real 'choice'. From this perspective there is choice only if the environmental constraints are in some sense loose. How the traditional or 'rational' model of management defines discovery, choice and action is summarised in Figure 10.

It has been recognised for a long time that it is possible to practise some approximation to this rational decision-making/monitoring control process only in conditions close to certainty – that is, in conditions in which information is relatively freely available and the outcomes or actions can be, at least approximately, predicted. Thompson and Tuden made this point in their 1959 study, as did H.A. Simon in his 1957 and 1960 publications. Others have reinforced the point since (most recently Mintzberg, 1994).

Nevertheless, this qualification as to the applicability of the planning model is generally ignored by consultants and managers alike, as they try to apply planning processes to highly uncertain situations. But there are alternative process models which shed light on how managers behave in uncertain conditions. These alternatives are based on the notions of visions, missions or shared ideologies, and trial-and-error action. The most prominent proponents of this way of understanding the processes of decision-making and control are Tom Peters and Robert Waterman, who published their management best-seller, *In Search of Excellence*, in 1982, and James Quinn, whose studies of process led him to propose a model, very much like that of Peters and Waterman, called 'logical incrementalism'. The Quinn studies appeared in 1978 and 1980. Recent studies in a similar vein include those by Peters (1987) and Hammer and Champy (1993).

Logical Incrementalism

Figure 11 summarises the definitions of discovery, choice and action from the perspective of 'logical incrementalism'. In this approach to management, the overall framework within which choices are made is established by the vision and the values that leaders 'persuade' others in the organisation to share. High levels of uncertainty, however, make it impossible to set out how the vision is to be realised. Instead of a plan, a process of trial-and-error action has to be undertaken in the form of small experiments, and their outcomes are then discovered. This, in turn, allows the organisation to learn from its experience, in the sense that this experience provides a guide to the next choice of small experiments. This process of learning from small experimental moves leads to the realisation of the vision (De Geus, 1988).

In the uncertain conditions assumed, however, there is unlikely to be consensus on each experiment. The choice must therefore be made through political means (Mintzberg, 1994, pp.200-01). The most powerful coalitions in the organisation or a charismatic (or just powerful) leader will determine with which strategic moves the organisation will experiment. Because all share (or are made to share) the same values and pursue the same vision, management becomes essentially a political process. The process involves 'bargaining', which is intended to proceed in a rather simple, stable and logical manner, rather than in a destabilising or disruptive way.

[52]

Figure 11: The Excellence Approach to Management

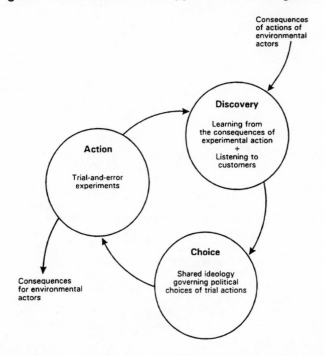

Quite clearly, then, this approach also involves negative feedback because there is intention as far as values and vision of a future state are concerned. The outcomes of small experiments are fed back into the choice process to keep the organisation moving towards the vision. Accordingly, Peters and Waterman, and Quinn, have proposed a version of what is essentially the planning model. Just as with that model, in the vision and values approach to management the development of an organisation is determined primarily by the choices managers make about long-term outcomes. Those choices are made by (hopefully) gifted individuals, who then employ political processes within the organisation to persuade others to share them. The result is stability and regularity, which is equated with success: the successful vision is the one which adapts an organisation to its environment. Hence, there is the same problem of 'real choice' as encountered with the rational model of managing.

Figure 12: Visionary/Ideological Form of Control

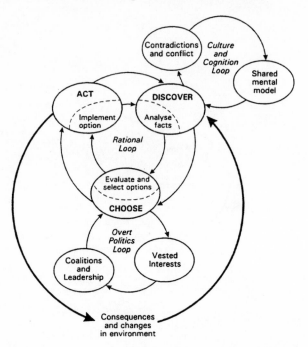

Integrating the Negative Feedback Model

The two models so far discussed are the ones that seem to dominate discussions about decision-making and control processes in management texts. In practice, however, it is clear that managers do not focus exclusively on one or the other. An integrated process model must therefore include both. Figure 12 shows how the discovery, choice and action feedback loop can be used to illustrate this process.

At the centre of the diagram is the rational decision-making and monitoring control loop presented in Figure 10. The next proposition, namely, that managers behave within a framework of shared ideology and vision, within a shared culture or recipe, is depicted by the culture and cognition loop in Figure 12. How and what a group of managers discovers about the actions of those that constitute their organisation's environment depends upon the mental models they share. When they strongly share the same models, they do not notice the contradictions and conflicts between their perception and what is happening. Thus they continue to act in a stable manner without questioning the culture or vision.

The trial-and-error, political form of decision-making can be taken into account by incorporating an overt 'politics loop'. This shows how choice is determined by leaders and stable coalitions within organisations which do not threaten vested interests because they choose within the accepted mental model of the environment they face.

The result is a model of organisational decision-making and control processes that focuses on information processing. This defines leadership in terms of setting clear or well-defined directions, articulating visions and cultures, and providing shape and logic to activities. In sum, it is defined in terms of managers *being in control.* Furthermore, all of the processes so far incorporated operate in a negative feedback manner:

O as managers move around the rational loop their monitoring activity keeps the organisation moving along a planned path;

O as managers move around the cognitive cultural loop, without changing the way they see the world, they keep responding in ways that can be predicted from past behaviour;

O as managers move around the political loop without threatening vested interests, because they all share the same culture, they keep the organisation moving towards a longer-term vision;

O after a crisis, organisations tend to revert to stable, conservative or equilibrium forms of behaviour until the next upheaval comes along.

It is quite clear, however, that life in organisations consists of more than these negative, stabilising feedback loops. We turn now to models that deal with positive or amplifying feedback in organisations.

Positive Feedback: Discovery, Choice and Action

As we saw in Chapter II, positive feedback is the opposite of negative feedback. Instead of feeding back the discrepancy between an outcome and an intention, so as to close the gap between the two, feedback progressively widens the gap. Positive feedback reinforces rather than cancels out deviations, and is therefore amplifying and destabilising. The creative rôle of conflict, dilemmas and tensions is now being noted by an increasing number of management specialists (Peters, 1987; Hampden-Turner, 1990; Pascale, 1990; Odiorne, 1991; Stacey, 1991 and 1992; Zimmerman and Hurst, 1992).

In practice, positive feedback is widespread in organisations and leads to self-reinforcing change. In Figure 12, consider managers going around a rational feedback loop at the centre of the diagram. Their discoveries about the world in which they operate and the manner in which they choose and act are all governed by a shared mental model or paradigm. Here they are practising Argyris and Schön's (1978) single-loop learning (see Chapter II, above, p.26). They are learning about the consequences of their behaviour and adjusting behaviour accordingly. But they are not questioning the frame of reference in which their learning takes place. Such single-loop learning is a negative feedback process leading to more stable behaviour.

However, where uncertainty and ambiguity increase, it becomes ineffective and dangerous to retain a mental model formulated and shared in conditions that have now changed. What is then required is double-loop learning. In this kind of learning, the shared mental model is questioned and changed. Double-loop learning has a destructive aspect in that it overturns the old outdated ways of perceiving. It also has a creative aspect insofar as it leads to a new mental map or paradigm.

The questioning of fundamental shared beliefs will arouse inevitable conflict within the organisation since vested interests will be threatened. Tensions occur when a crisis leads to a conflict of goals or means, perhaps even threatening the whole organisation's survival. Changes in ownership, macro-economic changes, new trade treaties, and so on, can all cause crises. In turbulent times, management can become incoherent and unable to cope with what is happening. Old hierarchical processes may have to be brushed away or side-stepped. New management may need to be imported to sweep the organisation clean. Informal networks or teams spring up which effectively replace the redundant formal procedures of decision-making.

Overt political activity is therefore no longer a simple bargaining process or top-down coercion used to select particular experimental actions. Instead, it is essentially a destabilising activity. The proponents of new perspectives, beliefs and mental models attempt to organise coalitions to support fundamental changes, sometimes including changes in leadership. Such political activity takes the form of positive feedback because individuals use it to amplify new issues and perspectives throughout the organisation. This can lead to unintended and unexpected outcomes.

Organisational Defence Routines

When people in an organisation experience uncertainty, ambiguity, questioning of fundamental beliefs, unexpected and unintended outcomes, conflict or contradiction, they also experience anxiety. There is a fear of failure and embarrassment. Argyris (1990) has shown how this leads to covert political behaviour, organisational defences, cover-ups and game-playing. The most usual and widespread form of the latter is to say one thing while doing another. This results in a gap between espoused and actual actions. The gap becomes undiscussable and the undiscussability itself becomes undiscussable. The effect of all this may be to protect people from the necessity to examine and question their mental models and so avoid the need for double-loop learning. If this happens, covert politics functions like negative feedback to sustain the *status quo*. On the other hand, game-playing can lead to vicious circles, chain reactions and bandwagon effects. These are all forms of feedback that destabilise an organisation. This in turn might provoke the questioning of fundamental beliefs and thus double-loop learning.

Unconscious Group Processes

Anxiety and fear of failure in organisational life, the inevitable consequences of high levels of uncertainty and ambiguity, can have even deeper consequences than simply provoking defence routines. Bion (1961) has shown that when people in a group become anxious, they show a strong tendency to regress to the forms of behaviour they used as infants. They do so to defend themselves against anxiety. He explained this by proposing that when people work together in a group, they do so within an emotional climate. So, a board of directors constitutes a sophisticated work group which works within a background emotional climate in which the directors accept (but not unquestioningly) the power of the chairman. When, however, they become anxious, the emotional climate suffuses the group and takes it over. This can block the ability to work effectively. For example, a board of directors may become so anxious that members stop thinking independently. They may simply do whatever the chairman wants.

Bion called this 'basic assumption behaviour'. Other examples of such basic assumptions are 'fight/flight' and 'pairing'. Under pairing, members of an organisation look to two of their number to provide the answers. Other writings on organisational life from a psycho-analytical perspective point to the unconscious defences people deploy to protect themselves from the anxieties of work (Anzieu, 1984; Hirschhorn, 1990). Such defences can take the form of ritualistic behaviour (Jacques, 1955; Menzies, 1975) or of fantasies that their organisation is all-powerful and perfect (Schwartz, 1990).

Unconscious group fantasies and basic assumption behaviour can operate in a negative feedback fashion to sustain the status quo. For example, people may have the narcissistic fantasy that their organisation can do no wrong. Or basic assumption behaviour may take the form of 'fight', which leads to amplifying and destabilising effects. The key point is that such unconscious fantasies and basic assumption behaviour are irremovable in organisations. They directly affect how people discover what is going on, and how they choose what to do. Ultimately, they determine how people act. Actions in organisations may often not be of the 'rational' type implicitly assumed in the planning literature. Using the same reasoning, the same is true of governments. Government policy may be far from 'rational', in the sense of being based on some sort of objective assessment of alternatives. Indeed, given the tensions of political life,

Figure 13: Self-Organisation

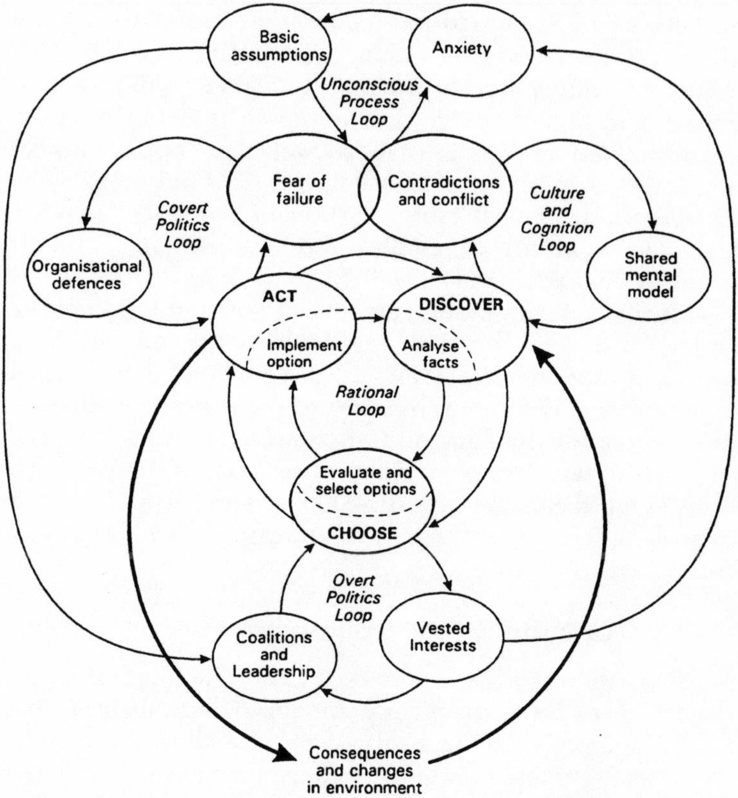

government decision-making may well be prone to group fantasies and basic assumption behaviour.

Integrating the Negative and Positive Feedback Models

Figure 13 adds the positive feedback loops so far discussed to present an integrated model of the strategy or policy-making process. The key point of the argument is that when managers are operating close to certainty – which normally means when they are conducting the repetitive day-to-day activities of their existing business – they are highly likely to operate within a shared mental model. This makes them feel secure and unafraid of failure. The rational loop at the centre of Figure 13 therefore dominates the whole process.

When managers are trying to do something innovative and creative, however, they question and change existing mental models. There is therefore something inherently destructive about creativity and innovation. The inevitable result is an increase in ambiguity, uncertainty, confusion, conflict, fear of failure and anxiety. It is also inevitable that the political, cognitive and unconscious loops will then operate in an amplifying manner, as discussed above. This will occur while in other respects – the organisation of day-to-day affairs – managers continue to employ the rational loop with its negative feedback effect.

A changeable, innovative, creative organisation is therefore bound to be one in which positive and negative feedback processes operate simultaneously. Thus the dynamics of organisational behaviour, in terms of the patterns of change, the degree of stability and instability or regularity and irregularity, are complex. They arise from amplifying and dampening feedbacks occurring at the same time. It is with such complexities that scientists studying chaos have been concerned.

Ordinary and Extraordinary Management

A group of managers operates at any one time within a shared 'paradigm' or mental model. For managers that paradigm is embodied in a particular hierarchical structure, a given set of rôles, a style of leadership, control, appraisal reward and other formal systems, missions, culture, ideology and business (for government, political) philosophy. This paradigm, the result of previous experience and learning, more or less dictates the objectives and strategies the managers of the organisation pursue. Their task is to solve the puzzle of how to carry out the strategy and to achieve the objectives. This can be thought of as *ordinary management*, a process of going around a puzzle-solving loop (as depicted on the right-hand side of Figure 14). Managers go around that loop using the rational process loop at the centre of Figure 13. The other loops are largely dormant because managers are operating within the certainty of the paradigm they share.

However, as managers go about ordinary management, solving puzzles within their shared paradigm, they inevitably uncover anomalies between what occurs and what they

Figure 14: Ordinary and Extraordinary Management

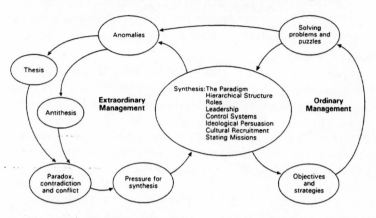

expect. All paradigms and shared mental models are only partial representations of reality. These anomalies build up to a point where managers begin to question their shared paradigm. When this occurs they embark upon what may be called *extraordinary management*. This is shown to the left in Figure 14. The key point is that the rational process loop cannot be used at all in the process of extraordinary management. Rational discourse presupposes a shared paradigm which is just what extraordinary management is in the process of destroying. It is the overt and covert politics, double-loop learning and unconscious process loops that are activated when managers practise extraordinary management.

The different processes managers must deploy when they practise ordinary and extraordinary management indicate the instruments they must use. The rational, culturally shared processes of ordinary management are pursued through the structures and systems of the formal organisation. But the processes deployed when extraordinary management is practised lie outside the formal organisation. An organisation is changeable when it operates in a way that leads to a contentious process of continually developing and dealing with an ever-changing agenda of issues.

The strategy process in firms is therefore dynamic and evolving. It is not a strategic intent that is held constant for many periods, as sometimes suggested. In organisations, self-organisation is the spontaneous formation of interest groups and coalitions around specific issues. It is through such groups that individuals promote an issue and by achieving a consensus the organisation embarks on a new strategy (*cf.* Nohria and Eccles, 1993). But this consensus disappears as the next issue arises. In this respect organisations are dissipative structures.

Chaos theory makes it difficult to avoid confronting the fundamentally paradoxical nature of management – that is, that managers must employ the rational loop within a shared mental model to operate efficiently when they are close to certainty. But they must also inevitably employ other processes that generate instability and shatter shared mental models, as a vital part of the process of change. Our argument emphasises the essentially disorderly and unplanned nature of strategic redirection and organisational transformation which takes place informally within a more orderly, hierarchical and planned system for dealing with day-to-day matters.

The Consequences for Decision-Making and Organisational Change

The argument so far can be summarised as follows. As with all other non-linear feedback systems, an organisation may be driven by negative feedback processes which sustain it in an adaptive fit with its *current* environment. The result is regular, orderly patterns of behaviour. The key to this regularity in human systems is the shared mental model. This shared view of the world sustains feelings of security and holds at bay the positive feedback processes which inevitably cause instability. The consequence of continuing to share the same mental model, however, is that innovation is impossible. The organisation can continue to build only on its existing strengths. There is now considerable evidence that this attraction to a 'stable point' leads to failure in competitive environments (Miller, 1990; Pascale, 1990; Handy, 1994). By their very nature, competitive environments change and change continuously.

However, as in other non-linear feedback systems, organisations can be driven predominantly by positive feedback. This takes the form of disruptive overt and covert political activity, defence mechanisms, game-playing and highly neurotic, unconscious processes and forms of leadership. Organisations dominated by such positive feedback processes are attracted to disintegration and ultimate failure (Miller and de Vries, 1987).

This suggests that, in order to survive and thrive, organisations must employ some combination of negative and positive feedback processes. This can happen in practice because of the different rôles of the formal and informal systems to be found in any organisation. When they are effective, the formal systems and structures of an organisation govern its repetitive day-to-day activities using negative feedback, thus allowing it to carry out efficiently its normal activities in a regular, predictable, planned and stable manner. But at the same time, people in an effective organisation operate within a richly connected and informal or decentralised system that embraces people across organisational boundaries.

It is in this informal system that positive feedback operates. The amplifying activities of double-loop learning, of covert games and unconscious processes, provoke people to learn in a constructive manner. *The behaviour pattern produced by this combination of negative and positive feedback processes has all the hallmarks of scientific chaos.* There are recognisable if irregular patterns in which unpredictable specific developments occur. There is a mixture of instability within stability or bounded instability.

We reach, then, one of the main insights chaos theory brings to organisations. In most of the management literature, the concept of 'managing change' is built on the idea that stability is desirable. The central organisational problem is seen as one of determining how to get from one state of stability to another when the environment changes. The idea that people can manage change assumes that there is a predictable end point, a point to which the organisation can move so as to return it to 'normal' or 'equilibrium'. The insights of chaos theory show just how limited this idea is. If we wish organisations to be innovative we have to accept that change is continuous. Results will be inherently unpredictable so that stability is only a chance, temporary phase. Planning innovative change then becomes impossible. Instead, 'changeability' must be built into the organisation. We have to establish and encourage the conditions within which organisations become changeable. Organisations (including governments) have to become skilled at influencing and adapting to continuous change.

[63]

Policies and Structures Must Allow for 'Creative Tension' to Thrive

What this means in terms of organisations' changing and adapting is as follows:

○ Creativity in organisations has an essentially destructive aspect. There can be no creation without destruction and the anxiety and disruption it can cause. Such destructiveness cannot occur when people share the same values or culture. So, on the one hand, there is a paradox that the efficient conduct of day-to-day business (or in government, policy) requires that people share a culture and have the same values. But on the other hand, creativity requires that these cultures and values must be constantly questioned. *Policies or business structures and systems that make it impossible for differences between people to flourish, that prevent a creative tension, block adaptability and innovation.*

○ In the management and government literature, change is often top-down driven. But how do top management or civil servants perceive the need to change or how to change (Doz and Prahalad, 1991, p.151)? Our argument is that *creativity emerges spontaneously* from the self-organising political and learning processes of people in organisations (also see Howard (ed.), 1993). The bounded instability required for creativity to develop leads to the disappearance of clear links between actions and long-term outcome. *This makes it impossible for anyone or any formal group in an organisation, such as 'corporate planners' or 'the Treasury', to plan or even envisage successfully, except in the most general of terms, the long-term future.*

○ Instead of choosing actions using the criterion of long-term outcome, the organisation should adopt actions which keep options open rather than close them down. *This implies a decentralised or fractal form of organisation in business and government which encourages the generation of information and adaptability* (Perry, Stott and Smallwood, 1993).

O Instead of planning strategy, managers should sow the
   seeds of innovation by throwing out challenges, by
   sustaining ambiguities and by creating the conditions
   within which people can spontaneously self-organise.
   Managers and policy-makers need to understand and
   rely upon emergent behaviour. What is required is the
   self-renewing organisation which engages in constant
   self-questioning and is open to new information
   (Pascale, 1990). *Destabilising information promotes
   innovation and change and must not be distorted or filtered out
   by the organisational bureaucracy or vested interests.*

The Decentralised Organisation and the Rôle of Markets

In recent years organisations have been examining their
processes and methods of working because of growing
competition. Improvement is at the core of 'total quality
management' programmes. Comparing process and performance against other firms is enshrined in the term 'bench-
marking'. 'Culture change' programmes in companies have a
longer pedigree going back to the 1970s. Now businesses are
being sold the idea of 're-engineering' the entire business
process in a management best-seller (Hammer and Champy,
1993). These reforms share an underlying assumption that
what determines an organisation's performance can be
identified and, in a purposeful way, acted upon.[3] They appear

---

[3] Hammer and Champy in their book on company 're-engineering' are
concerned, rightly, with the *processes* by which companies operate. They are
aware of the need for processes to adapt and change. In that sense their
approach and our approach are complementary. However, they are seemingly
unwilling to let go of the idea that somehow there is an optimal process that
can be planned or designed. Their approach still has, therefore, a link with
the rational tradition of strategic planning which we reject. For example, they
write (p.100): 'Building a strategy around what [technology] one can buy in
the market today means that a company will always be playing catch up with
competitors who have already anticipated it. These competitors know what
they are *going* to do with the technology *before* it becomes available, so they will
be ready to deploy it when it becomes available' (their emphasis). The idea
that a business can know what it is going to do with a technology that has not
yet appeared is patently absurd. But our criticism of their approach goes
further than this. We would argue that a firm cannot know at the outset what it
will *ultimately* do even with an *existing* technology. For example, the potential
of cable technology for all kinds of communication and information flows is
only slowly emerging.

to discount the idea that in practice it is not possible to know with any kind of certainty what method of working will be optimal for the *future* competitive environment.

The only sensible response to relentless change in the world economy is relentless adaptation and improvement at the organisational level, not one-off or intermittent management purges (Peters, 1987). The economic environment is becoming more competitive for most organisations as it becomes more global. Continuously faster technological change and increasingly demanding customers add further pressures. Chaos theory emphasises discontinuous change and self-organisation, creative destruction and renewal, and inherently unpredictable outcomes.

In terms of strategic management and government this implies the design of organisational processes that can *continually* generate novelty and adaptability. It suggests a shift of focus from ends or outcomes, as in the traditional or 'rational' approach to management, towards the means or process. Organisational structures and processes at the business and government levels should concentrate on the removal of the constraints that limit adaptability. It is self-evident that commercial enterprises operating in competitive markets must be continually innovating or they will not survive. A bigger problem exists for organisations not normally exposed to competitive market forces, such as non-profit-making institutions, state agencies and churches.

Nothing can remove 'unknowability'. It follows, therefore, that if an organisation is operating in the border area between stability and instability, as it must be if it is to be innovative, decision-making processes that entail forecasting or making firm assumptions about future states are very likely to be ineffective. Consequently, the long-term future of organisations and economies should not be planned in any formal sense, though in their repetitive day-to-day activities both organisations and parts of economies (public spending, monetary policy, and so on) have to be 'planned'. Instead, organisations and economies should be made inherently changeable. The focus, then, is on creativity and entrepreneurship as well as on bureaucracy and short-term planning methods. Managing organisations and economies is a paradoxical matter in which one approach necessarily conflicts with the other.

Managers and policy-makers need to find innovative solutions to what are usually complex and very ill-understood problems, all the time operating in a highly uncertain and chaotic world. There can be no prescriptive or general solutions. Indeed, a set of specific prescriptions of the type 'Ten Ways to Certain Success' will lead to almost certain failure. Management will become locked in to methods and a mental map that must, even if appropriate at the time, become highly inappropriate over time (Miller, 1990). Managers need continuously and imaginatively to review their organisations, the paradigm and culture that determine actions, and not least how they themselves think and behave. There is a need for management to 'flip' into a new way of thinking much like the bifurcations in nature (*cf.* Morgan, 1993). This is far from being a mechanistic process. It requires considerable mental agility and accompanying organisational flexibility – an organisational environment that encourages the generation and diffusing of information regarding opportunities and resource costs.

Chaos theory highlights the need to create rather than simply process information. In this sense it provides a powerful case for enterprise. Non-equilibrium conditions are sustained only provided there is a continuing input of energy into the system. This is especially true of systems which are far from equilibrium, as recent scientific research has indicated. To combat stultifying bureaucracy, organisations should continuously promote constructive tension, achieved through a constant questioning of the *status quo* (which is what enterprise is all about). In market economies, enterprise provides a vital input of energy through new products and processes which create a positive feedback process leading to spontaneous change. The creativity of entrepreneurial innovation is the means through which market economies adjust and adapt. It is the engine by which the future of the market economy emerges. We have more to say about enterprise in the discussion of the complementary nature of Austrian economics and chaos theory in Chapter IV (below, p.88).

Creating interaction with the environment through the competitive market enhances the self-renewing aspect of organisations. Bureaucracy and established processes are challenged, for example, by subjecting the organisation to the pressures of a competitive market and the new products and methods of production generated by enterprise. Organisations protected from competition are much less likely to change and adapt because the pressures to do so are avoided.

Public Sector Organisations More Resistant to Change

Where competition is limited, as it often is in the public sector, we should expect organisations to be more resistant to change and hence more static, more conservative and concerned with an equilibrium or stable state. This is supported by rules and regulations, traditional systems and traditional ways of working. In other words, the public sector is dominated by negative rather than positive feedback processes. The predominant form of learning is single loop. There is little questioning of the mode of working or the way things are done. When work pressures rise, the response is to demand more resources to continue to perform to the same standard and in the same way. One way of breaking out of this mind-set and of promoting fundamental change is to expose the organisation to competition. There is no guarantee that this will work, but at least organisations that do not adapt will fail and be replaced by more efficient suppliers.

In the public sector this has been approached in recent years through privatisation and deregulation. Privatisation should subject organisations to the disciplines of the capital and product markets. Where this has not been deemed feasible, competitive tendering for the right to be the monopoly supplier has been used (Parker, 1994). Where competition remains limited, however, over the longer term the pressure to change must be continuous. In the absence of new 'energy' all organisations, being dissipative structures, can be expected to return to a static equilibrium.

The need to increase productivity, flexibility and cost control is already leading to fundamental changes in business organisation and employment patterns in the private sector. Over the last five years alone, more than 90 per cent of the largest organisations in the UK have restructured. Many of these expect to restructure again in the next few years (*Professional Manager*, November 1993, p.5). In organisations

[68]

operating in competitive markets, adaptation is encouraged by an effective flow of timely information regarding consumer wants and resource costs. This tells against hierarchical and bureaucratic forms of management, in particular, and favours the use of internal prices and decentralised management structures (cf. Halal, 1986; Dumaine, 1991; Halal, Geranmayeh and Proudehnad, 1993) – what Gable and Ellig (1993) call 'market-based management'. This helps explain why the favoured forms of re-organisation of late have entailed the cutting out of tiers of middle management ('de-layering') and introducing separate business units as cost or profit centres.

As the pace of change in the international economy accelerates, so must the organisation's ability to adapt if it is to survive. In the past, high levels of decentralisation were resisted because of the difficulty of controlling the organisation's aggregate finances. This problem has now been reduced by major advances in information technology which allow central financial control of a large number of independent units.

The Era of Self-Organisation?

In a real sense we are leaving behind the age of organised organisations and moving into an era where the need is for processes of self-organisation. Informal networks within the firm and similar forms of teamwork and clusters enable taken-for-granted assumptions regarding methods of working to be explored and challenged. It has been recognised for a long time, for instance, that Japanese industry relies for process improvements on the workers who operate on the assembly line and not simply on formal management (Nonaka, 1993). However, chaos is a paradoxical state of both stability and instability. This is reflected in the need for hierarchies and planning systems, to carry out existing day-to-day activities efficiently, and *at the same time* to have loose, informal, destabilising networks to promote change.

Ronald Coase suggested in 1937 that business firms exist to reduce transactions costs – the costs in market exchanges of searching for suppliers and customers, of contract bargaining, and of monitoring expenses relating to ensuring quality in delivery and enforcing agreements. At the same time, however, it is now well recognised that organising economic

[69]

activity within firms involves parallel costs (Williamson and Winter (eds.), 1991) relating to the management of resources to prevent waste or 'slacking' and the threat of growing bureaucracy.

To minimise these costs, a key task of management is to establish systems that facilitate adaptation and economy. It is perhaps not surprising, therefore, that in the private sector 'outsourcing' peripheral functions is gaining ground. So is the use of internal pricing (Lacity and Hirshheim, 1993). Internal markets can help to de-bureaucratise the firm, providing internal suppliers and customers with the information and incentives to make profitable decisions, whilst reducing overhead costs (Ellig, 1993, p.25).

Like a market economy, a market-based firm is decentralised and based upon a continuous generation of information about resource costs and customer demands. Profitability plays an important rôle as a measure of divisional performance. Unprofitable activities are identified and can be eliminated. Hierarchies and rigid chains of command are minimised. Each business unit is linked to a number of other units in the firm through prices rather than top-down dictate (Cowen and Ellig, 1993). Business teams form and disband when necessary, aiding extraordinary management which is the key to strategic change.

To sum up, in such firms the structure and processes within the organisation emphasise the discovery, dissemination and integration of knowledge within the firm. Change does not have to be externally imposed through some 'cultural change' or 're-engineering' programme. Instead, a tension leading to continuous adaptation and learning is built into the organisation's structure. It becomes more fractal-like as incentives to adapt become part of the organisation.

Only the adaptable firm that is based on 'real time' learning and speedy reaction – the firm that is inherently flexible – can contend with the unknowable future. Such firms successfully operate with a combination of both ordinary and extraordinary management. In other words, it is such firms that operate with bounded instability, like creative systems in nature. The same reasoning can be applied to the study of successful economies.

[70]

IV. THE COMPLEX, EVOLVING ECONOMY

'The bane of political economy has been the haste of its students to possess themselves of a complete and symmetrical system, solving all the problems before it with mathematical certainty and exactness. The very attempt shows an entire misconception of the nature of those problems, and of the means available for their solution.'

(T.E.C Leslie, 1879, p.241)

Economic relationships are embodied in feedback loops. Decisions by economic agents (firms, households and governments) affect the economic environment, which in turn affects further economic decisions. Economic argument usually proceeds on the basis that economic feedbacks are mainly negative and can be expressed by linear equations. Consequently, markets move smoothly and quickly towards an equilibrium. There they remain until another change comes along. In reality, however, economic feedbacks can also be positive and non-linear, leading to considerable instability.

Chaos and Economics

In evaluating the significance of chaos theory for the study of economies, the first question to be asked is whether, in practice, economic relationships produce chaotic behaviour? This has not proved an easy question to answer because of the difficulty of teasing out random from non-random events in economic data. Economies are constantly changing and it is no small matter to identify which changes are determined within the system ('endogenous') and which are the result of stochastic or random external 'shocks' ('exogenous'). In a time-series subject to chaotic dynamics, it is very easy to attribute motions either to structural change in the economic model, when in fact there is no change, or (equally erroneously) to attribute them to random disturbances.

Research has been conducted at two broad levels. Although it is not the purpose of this *Hobart Paper* to review the results in detail, it is useful to refer to them briefly (for more detailed reviews see, for example, Baumol and Benhabib, 1989, and Boldrin and Woodford, 1990). The research has been concerned both with developing theoretical models which show that chaos can arise in economic relationships and with the search for chaos in time-series data.

At the theoretical level, studies have shown that chaos can occur where there are appropriate combinations of lags and non-linearity and that such conditions may arise in many areas of economic life, including money supply and production, inventory cycles, strategic decision-making in firms, business cycles and growth models, technological innovation, duopoly competition, productivity growth, and research and development and advertising expenditures.[1] Day (1983) uses a Malthusian model of the economy, where the rate of population growth is determined by the level of output and output is itself dependent on the size of the labour force. He shows that the feedback loop can result in either cycles or chaos. Indeed, Day points out that Thomas Malthus may have been one of the first economists to stumble on the essence of chaotic dynamics. In 1817, Malthus wrote:

'A faithful history ... would probably prove the existence of retrograde and progressive movements ... [that] ... must necessarily be rendered irregular' (Malthus, 1817, p.91).

There is no shortage of theoretical models containing the conditions which could lead to chaos. The empirical literature is, however, much more limited in nature, largely because of the need for big data sets if chaos is to be

---

1 In more detail, the theoretical studies are: monetary aggregates (Cunningham, 1990); inventory cycles (Medio, 1991); strategic decision-making in firms (Richards, 1990); exchange rates (Krugman, 1991; Pesaran and Samiei, 1992); overlapping-generation equilibrium models of the economy (e.g. Benhabib and Day, 1980 and 1982; Grandmont, 1985 and 1986); business cycles and growth models (Day, 1982 and 1983; Dana and Malgrange, 1984; Day and Walter, 1989); employment (Burgess, 1993); technological innovations (Deneckere and Judd, 1986; Goodwin, 1986; Arthur, 1989); the Keynesian model (Day and Shafer, 1985); duopoly competition (Rand, 1978); productivity growth (Baumol and Wolf, 1983); research and development spending (Baumol and Benhabib, 1989); and advertising expenditure (Baumol and Quandt, 1985).

identified.[2] The shortness of most economic time-series means it is difficult to distinguish chaotic turbulence from motions in the data resulting from stochastic factors or 'noise'. Nevertheless, despite major data problems, a number of studies have confirmed the existence of the necessary (though not sufficient) condition for chaos, significant non-linearity. Such non-linearity has been found in series relating to monetary aggregates, foreign exchange rates, employment and industrial and pig iron production, mergers and acquisitions, American work stoppages, gold and silver markets, stock market and bond prices, and some GNP and GDP data. These results have to be balanced against those from studies that have reported contradictory results or no evidence of likely chaos. Such results have come from, for example, studies of European and North American GNP and Canadian unemployment data.[3]

Where the conditions for chaos have not been found, though this could be because of data limitations, it may be because the methods of testing for chaos are not especially well developed (Scheinkman, 1990; Bullard and Butler, 1993). They are especially stretched where there are both chaotic and stochastic influences present at the same time.[4]

---

[2] McCaffrey et al. (1992) have introduced a new approach for discovering chaos in which smaller sample sizes can be accommodated. As yet, however, the method is largely untested.

[3] The following empirical studies find evidence of non-linearity which could conceivably lead to chaos: monetary aggregates (Barnett and Chen, 1986; Chen, 1988; De Coster and Mitchell, 1991); foreign exchange rates (Park, 1991; Medio, 1992); employment, industrial production and pig iron production (Brock and Sayers, 1988; Terasvirta and Anderson, 1993); merger and acquisition activity (Town, 1993); American work stoppage data (Sayers, 1986); gold and silver markets (Frank and Stengos, 1987 and 1989); stock market and bond prices (Scheinkman and LeBaron, 1989; Peters, 1991 and 1994; Cao and Tsay, 1993); and GNP and GDP data (Scheinkman and LeBaron, 1987; Frank, Gencay and Stengos, 1988). The studies which have reported contradictory results or no evidence of likely chaos include: on US GNP data (Broch and Sayers, 1988); British, Italian and West German GNP figures (Frank, Gencay and Stengos, 1988); and Canadian national income and unemployment data (Frank and Stengos, 1988b). Also, Hsieh (1989, 1991) attributes the variance in exchange rates and stock returns mainly to factors other than chaotic dynamics.

[4] Almost all chaotic models in economics have employed one-dimensional (single-variable, first-order) difference equations. But chaos is more likely to arise in higher-order (higher-dimension) systems.

Also, chaotic motions can be associated with intermittent turbulence. Hence a failure to discover chaos in a set of time-series data could be a function of the time-period selected, especially where short data runs are used. It may also be relevant that a number of the empirical studies giving the most promising results for chaos theory have been based on financial data where there are longer runs. They are also less aggregated than GNP or employment data and are therefore less prone to pollution by 'noise'.

In summary, the evidence on the existence of chaos in economies is far from conclusive. It does seem, however, that economic activity is associated with significant non-linearity and that, consequently, economic behaviour can be highly complex and unpredictable. Even where there appears to be a long-run trend in data, important shorter-term fluctuations can appear which undermine useful prediction for economic policy purposes. The timing of shifts from trend becomes unpredictable, and there cannot therefore be high confidence that an existing trend will continue.

What seems clear is that economic time-series data do show complex and sometimes unexpected motions which are difficult to explain in terms of traditional economic theory (see Baumol, 1987, for an example concerned with US labour productivity data). We consider below the key implications for economics of chaotic dynamics, based on the belief that such ideas can usefully contribute to an understanding of economic behaviour. We start by examining econometric modelling and forecasting.

The Implications for Modelling and Forecasting

The problems caused for econometric modelling by random shocks, which by their nature are unpredictable, are well rehearsed. Chaotic dynamics provide another powerful argument against placing much if any reliance on forecasting from econometric models, because of the nature of the statistical methods used and because of the essentially unknowable nature of chaotic futures.

The most widely used statistical techniques in economic forecasting assume that deviations of actual variables from the average are normally distributed. This is not usually a particularly significant limitation. Under chaotic conditions, however, system behaviour is neither normally distributed nor regular. Therefore, in the presence of chaos, regression and similar statistical methods are of doubtful value in deriving relationships. Chaos theory also highlights the need to include all relevant variables when studying an economic problem: where chaos exists, for accurate forecasts to be made all of the relevant parameters would have to be both *known* and *perfectly specified*. This is crucial because of the state in chaos known as 'sensitive dependence'. Where the system is boundedly unstable, tiny differences in equation specification or in input data can lead to very different economic forecasts.

In practice, errors are usual in statistical analyses, which are universally based on sampling procedures. Errors arise during both data collection and analysis. Moreover, it is normal procedure to round economic data in econometric models. But under conditions of chaos, in some cases even a variation to a number of decimal places can completely alter the behaviour of the system. Before the subject of chaotic dynamics was explored this was not recognised. In economic forecasting, minor statistical errors introduced during data collection and analysis were presumed to cause only a minor variation in the prediction.

Under conditions of chaos, tiny errors are strongly amplified: forecasts can be wildly inaccurate even when the model is correctly specified and there are no random shocks to disturb the system. Moreover, where shocks do occur, even the smallest change in parameter values can drastically alter the behaviour of the system (Schuster, 1989).

When an event is exogenous it is not part of the defined system. But in an economy with complex interrelationships and feedbacks this is a critical limitation of the model. In the presence of chaotic dynamics it is essential to build economic models which include all relevant economic relationships, no matter how insignificant they may seem. But this is beyond the capability (and imagination) of the model builder since it is not possible to know which are the relevant relationships until after the event. Macro-economic models typically contain hundreds or thousands of parameters and it would be astonishing if errors did not exist sufficient, in the presence of chaos, to rule out confidence in the predictions. In effect, to build a reliable econometric model of the economy to predict a chaotic future we would need to be given that future in advance!

To date there has been more interest by researchers in the presence of chaos at the macro-economic than at the micro-economic level, though there is no obvious reason to believe that chaos is less relevant to micro-economics (Town, 1993). Chaotic dynamics cast doubt not only on the value of macro-economic forecasting but on using past company or industry data to forecast future costs, demand relationships, outcomes of advertising campaigns, and so on. Management may take comfort in planning the future using quantitative forecasts. It is perhaps not surprising, however, that despite the growing sophistication of the models used, firms apparently continue to fail at more or less the same rate as before.

Pattern Recognition

The fact that chaos questions the value of econometric modelling for forecasting purposes must come as unwelcome news to many economists. It does not necessarily mean, however, that economists can have nothing useful to say about economic outcomes. Fortunately, although the behaviour of chaotic systems can appear random, there is a hidden order. Just as we know that a mongrel puppy will grow into a dog and not a cat, so we can draw broad boundaries around feasible results in economies, even though we may not be able to predict definite outcomes. For example, prices do not suddenly explode; the economy will neither collapse nor completely transform in the short term; and industries do not disappear over-night (though they can disappear quickly, as happened in the case of the British motor-cycle industry).

Similarly, history shows that economies go through typical cycles of recovery, boom, recession and recovery. We cannot necessarily predict the size of the output swings, the implications for employment, productivity and prices, or the timing of each stage of the cycle. But we can predict a broad pattern to business cycles. The most basic of concepts in economics, demand and supply in the competitive market, is associated with a pattern of behaviour leading to price movements. When supply exceeds demand a price reduction is likely, though it is usually tricky to predict the precise reduction. Price movements are described by a pattern that results from the behaviour of markets. Similar patterns can be found in inflationary conditions, labour markets, exchange rates, and so on.

In chaotic markets, patterns of behaviour will be irregular but bounded. The time-path of an economic variable may be aperiodic and never reach the same point twice in any defined period. Normally, however, the time-path will not entail continuous expansion or contraction. The behaviour of economic agents is such as to provide, as it were, 'attractors' (see Chapter II, p.29) holding the movement of economic variables within bounds. For example, aggregate demand does not shrink continuously since price changes act to restore demand after a certain point. Similarly, investment is not continuously expanded since there comes a point at which there is excess supply. In financial markets the behaviour of speculators is such as to inhibit linear-like bull or bear markets. Hence, economic movements are complex but not completely unstable. In this respect, economic behaviour exhibiting chaotic dynamics can be distinguished from behaviour following a random path. Very broad patterns of behaviour may be discernible for a while, provided there is no reason to believe there has been a fundamental change of structure in the economy or market studied. Random movements, by definition, follow no discernible pattern.

In sum, chaos theory suggests that while economic forecasting and econometric model-building are at best hazardous pursuits, this does not rule out useful observations about economic relationships. We know there is a pattern to demand and supply movements. When demand exceeds supply in a competitive market, price can be expected to rise. When a particular type of skilled labour is in short supply, we can expect the wage for such labour to increase. In both cases the price or wage rise can be expected to lead over time to an increase in supply of the product or type of labour.

Equally, at the macro-economic level there are similar patterns of events. For example, an over-valued exchange rate can be expected to depress export sales and encourage imports. A large budget deficit in a fully employed economy can be expected to lead to inflation.

These basic relationships are part of the 'tool kit' of economic analysis. Chaos theory does not question such relationships. What it does question is the idea that these relationships can be quantified with any real precision so that a *precise* outcome can be predicted. The failure to understand the difference between comprehension or explanation and prediction lies behind the weakness of much economics teaching today. It also helps to explain the failure of governments when they try to smooth out business cycles with economic 'fine tuning'.

Endogenous and Chaotic Fluctuations

The source of the economic fluctuations that are termed business cycles and the optimal policy response to them continue to be controversial (Zarnowitz, 1985; Gabisch and Lorenz, 1988). In broad terms, the on-going and lively debate about macro-economic policy between neo-Keynesians ('orthodox' and 'post-Keynesian' varieties) on the one hand, and monetarist and neo-classical economists on the other, arises from opposing beliefs about the source of economic fluctuations and hence how to react to them. One approach argues that the economy is essentially stable or in equilibrium. Fluctuations result from stochastic factors. An early study in this mould was produced by Frisch (1933) and this view continues to be favoured by many economists. Economic fluctuations are still attributed to shocks, such as an oil price increase, unanticipated actions of the fiscal and monetary authorities or (more recently) the ending of the Cold War – despite the fact that empirical confirmation is often lacking.

The other broad approach to business cycles argues that there is no inherent reason why a market economy should be stable. In other words, economic fluctuations are endogenous. Today the idea that cycles might arise from the internal dynamics of a market economy is rooted mainly in Keynesian economics. Keynes in *The General Theory* talked about the possibility of insufficient demand leading to general unemployment. He also talked about the impact of uncertainty and unpredictable 'animal spirits' on investment.

Chaos theory offers an alternative explanation for endogenous economic fluctuations. Provided there is sufficient non-linearity in the economic system, chaos can arise in Keynesian and non-Keynesian models of the economy alike (see, for instance, Benhabib and Day, 1982; Day and Shafer, 1985). Interestingly, non-linear models of the trade cycle were used earlier this century, for example by Kaldor in 1940, Hicks in 1950 and Goodwin in 1951 (Scheinkman, 1990,

[78]

p.33). Also, Lundberg in 1937 and Samuelson in 1939 set about explaining business cycles using models in which the results were sensitive to changes in the parameters (Baumol and Benhabib, 1989, p.78). However, these models generated regular (limit) cycles which did not fit well with experience. Consequently, they were replaced by linear equation systems. The economy was modelled as essentially stable and growing; irregular cycles were attributed to exogenous shocks.

The Business Cycle Puzzle

Trade fluctuations are puzzling because they appear to be partly regular and partly erratic. Chaos theory provides a plausible explanation. It demonstrates that a complex time-path for the economy can exist containing abrupt and random-like changes over time, which can produce oscillations that are difficult to predict, albeit within a bounded region. The need for random shocks to explain business cycles is eliminated, though this is not to argue that outside shocks are necessarily unimportant nor that all macroeconomic fluctuations are necessarily explained by chaos.

An awareness that economic fluctuations may be caused by endogenous factors arising from chaotic dynamics, as well as from external shocks, is important for an informed discussion of economic policy. Chaotic dynamics provide an explanation of *endogenous turbulence** in economies. This means the economy will not necessarily be stable even in the absence of shocks. Moreover, where a shock (such as an oil price increase or an unanticipated government policy change) causes a sudden adjustment in the economy, an economic system that returns quickly and smoothly to equilibrium will cope easily with it. Non-linear systems are sensitive-dependent and the shock effect may be highly magnified under chaotic behaviour.

Rational Expectations

The idea that the economy is essentially stable and settles into a smoothly growing time-path in the absence of shocks is central to the new classical critique of Keynesian economics which starts from the premise of rational expectations. Most rational expectations theorists follow Robert Lucas (1975 and 1981) in assuming that, while economic agents may not have perfect foresight when making plans, they use all available information to come to the best possible forecasts of the future. They may make mistakes when forming expectations, but there should be no persistent forecasting errors. This means that deviations from full employment are transitory. They are caused from time to time by exogenous shocks, such as technology changes or higher oil prices, which are temporarily misperceived in markets or that trigger delays in capital stock adjustment. Where there is a sequence of random shocks, the economy behaves in a way that resembles a business cycle.

Rational expectations theory is fundamentally questioned by chaos (Kelsey, 1988, p.22). The theory accepts imperfect information, but in the presence of true uncertainty, as implied by chaos, people cannot have a coherent model of the world and expectations will diverge. In general, in the presence of chaotic dynamics they would not be able to predict optimal outcomes with any reliability. They would therefore be unable to form rational expectations of the future of the type proposed by rational expectations theory. Where chaos exists, agents do not learn accurately and there can be no perfect foresight. In an environment of non-linear feedbacks and reaction time-lags, it is rational not to hold firm expectations of future outcomes. In consequence, behaviour may lead to endogenous cycles and aperiodic motions, just as Keynesian economics predicts.

The Management of Demand: A Keynesian Dead End

Not surprisingly, the conclusion that under chaotic conditions the competitive market economy can produce instability leading to unemployment has been seized upon by neo-Keynesians eager to grasp the initiative from the rational expectations school. If the competitive market is unstable after all, they argue, government should intervene to create stability. In an especially influential study, Grandmont (1985) concluded that monetary policy could be effective in reducing the irregular cycles caused by chaos (also see Brock and Malliaris, 1989, and Woodford, 1989).

Grandmont's reasoning is complex, but is essentially concerned with government making inter-generational money transfers to affect expectations of interest rates and real money balances. There is no need, however, to dwell on the theoretical content of the analysis because the resulting policy recommendation is of doubtful value. For policy purposes Grandmont's argument breaks down. Although chaos theory provides an explanation for fluctuations in a market economy, it also demonstrates that the state lacks *the knowledge* needed to adopt the correct counter-cyclical measures. As the chance of getting to a planned end-state is extremely low in a chaotic world, it is difficult to see how a government could specify a policy that would achieve the desired outcome, except perhaps by chance (Rosser, 1990, p.279).

Even though the competitive market economy is unstable, state intervention is unlikely to provide a solution. Indeed, it could be harmful because of the condition of sensitive dependence. In the absence of the ability to forecast the future, small errors in policy, in terms of the type or timing of state intervention, are almost certain to lead to highly magnified distortions. Instead of state intervention dampening down economic cycles, chaos theory helps us to understand why it may actually aggravate them.

Markets and Planning

The paradigm of the 'far from equilibrium organisation', discussed in Chapter III, has important implications for our understanding of markets. There are persuasive reasons for arguing that if business organisations wish to be innovative, they should strive to operate on the chaos frontier. Organisations which are attracted to integration and dull consensus forms of management tend to ossify and die. Those which over-encourage differentiation and conflict can become explosively unstable and break down. As we argued earlier, success seems to lie in operating in the border region or region of bounded instability. To achieve this outcome, constant management attention, information and entrepreneurial energy are required.

The same appears to be true of economies. A dynamic economy, like a dynamic firm, must be flexible and open to unanticipated (and 'unanticipatable') change. It must provide an economic and social environment conducive to adaptation. As Miller states:

'Much as we like to believe that "reality" is permanent, it is no more than a social construct – what we currently believe to be real. In a rapidly changing environment, these constructs require continual questioning. That will not happen simply through an orderly rational process: it needs imagination, intuition, fantasy, argument, disagreement, conflict.' (Miller, 1993, p.114)

Every firm, and for that matter every household, has its own peculiar history arising from differences in initial events, subsequent developments and occasional external or exogenous shocks. Hence an economy is made up of economic agents each pursuing their own distinctive if possibly chaotic trajectories or time-paths (Arthur, 1990). Firms and households react differently to economic events depending upon their precise circumstances and perceptions. The differences in behaviour may seem insignificant at the time, but over the longer term they can lead to widely differing outcomes. Where relationships are highly complex there will be few simple and reliable A-leads-to-B connections to draw on.

In chaotic systems the issue is not simply what are the answers; the main difficulty is knowing the questions. In the face of uncertainty, we cannot know what we do not know.[5] This suggests that, in reviewing the relative merits of economic institutions, the study should be conducted according to *which institutional form (or forms) is best able to contend with an unknowable future.* Human economic progress implies operation under conditions of bounded knowledge and imperfect reaction. Even where information about the future exists, economic agents have limited cognitive abilities and this affects the absorption and interpretation of information and consequent actions. The institutional form that best assists economic agents in achieving solutions to economic problems will therefore be one that is interactive and spontaneously self-organising, that generates information, enables agents to learn and adapt as they go along, and encourages entrepreneurial innovation and change (*cf.* Richardson, 1960).

Chaos, State Planning and Markets

In the debate over the relative merits of state planning and markets, the existence of chaos adds an important new dimension. To be successful, state planning requires an accurate knowledge of both the future and the means to

---

[5] There is a very useful discussion of this point in Israel Kirzner's *Discovery and the Capitalist Process*, Chicago: University of Chicago Press (1985).

achieve the desired ends. It requires clarity about causal relationships and goals and an ability to forecast the future without which planning is directionless. But as we have seen, where behaviour is chaotic there can be no certainty about causal relationships or even about optimal long-term objectives.

The long-term future cannot be reliably planned. Moreover, the costs of operating the planning system are directly related to the complexity of the economic environment which is to be planned, while additional economic costs are imposed when the adaptability of firms to their changing environment is reduced by state intervention. In consequence, central planning runs a high risk of reducing change and adaptation and of becoming ever more complex and costly as planners battle to retain some semblance of being in control. Certainly, the outcome of decades of planning in Central and Eastern Europe was increased bureaucratic confusion, restricted adaptation and, ultimately, economic stagnation compared with the market economies of the West.

By contrast to planned systems, markets encourage adaptability. Markets seem to cope well with the uncertainty and ambiguity inherent in modern, complex economies. Markets facilitate the creation of new knowledge and the double-loop learning on which innovation and economic progress depend. In a chaotic world, new knowledge starts with the individual and cannot be centrally designed or planned. In a market economy, knowledge is transmitted across the economy by market signals. Market signals act as effective signposts to potentially profitable new investment.

The market is a form of self-organisation that has proved adept at coping with the uncertainty inherent in economic life. In markets outcomes emerge; they are not planned by some central body. The market combines flexibility and control, both of which must exist if economies are to operate in the bounded instability region.

Markets are flexible, reactive and proactive with the environment. They facilitate change in the face of uncertainty. They are integrated with and encourage the necessary feedbacks between economic agents in an unpredictable world. They produce what F.A. Hayek aptly called 'spontaneous interaction' (Hayek, 1948, p.79). Of course, adaptability is maximised where there is competition.

[83]

Adaptation is much less likely to happen in a monopolistic market, where competitive pressures to change are removed, whether it is supplied by private sector firms or by government.

Government and the Economy

Government is not simply a question of pulling levers to obtain predictable, welfare-maximising outcomes. The 'public choice' literature has drawn attention in recent years to government failure resulting from the self-interested behaviour of those employed in the state machine. Moreover, it has highlighted the undue influence of special interest groups in policy-making (see, for example, Mitchell, 1988). But even where a government genuinely attempts to pursue the public interest and miraculously escapes capture by pressure groups, the existence of complex relationships means that it is most unlikely to adopt welfare-maximising policies because it will simply lack the knowledge to do so. Chaotic economies are inherently unknowable.

Chaotic economies are subject to unexpected change and the anxiety and disorientation it causes. While it is understandable that governments want to reduce the social and economic costs of change, it is essential that policies are not introduced which damage the capacity of economies to adapt creatively. Law and order and defence are essential to prevent explosive instability in society. State expenditures on education and training can be justified in terms of improving the abilities of the labour force to adapt. Even industrial subsidies, provided they promote innovation rather than simply prop-up the sleepy, can assist economies from time to time to change, though chaos helps to explain why industrial policy based on 'picking winners' is prone to failure.

The sort of subsidy policy most compatible with a chaotic economy is one in which governments do not attempt to plan the future and direct investment. Instead they encourage a competitive search for new markets and new methods of working. An example of this is the way the Japanese government has promoted industrial growth by encouraging inter-firm co-operation in developing new technologies, but has relied upon competition for the commercial exploitation of the product. By so doing the government promotes the process of competitive innovation rather than endeavouring to plan or predict precise outcomes: 'The ferocity of the competition strengthens efficiency and the international competitiveness of Japanese firms' (Okimoto, 1989, p.107).

At the same time, experience suggests that maintaining a heavily taxed and regulated economy discourages economic development by reducing investment and innovation. High taxes and regulation limit the economy's ability to change. They can push economies away from the border region towards a stable (static) point or state of stagnation.

Turning specifically to social policy, the conclusions to which chaos theory leads are far from simple. Society is a means of shaping individual behaviour within certain bounds determined by law, convention and ethical or moral norms. These laws, conventions and norms act, as it were, like attractors holding individual behaviour within certain understood limits: for example, 'thou shall not kill or steal'. In business dealings, fraud and other dishonest or unethical behaviour are viewed as unacceptable. Such shared values, including trust, are necessary for people to contract with each other and take part in market exchanges (Casson, 1991). In other words, laws, conventions and agreed norms of behaviour are necessary for market economies to function. Indeed, they are necessary if society is not to explode, leading to social and economic breakdown.

Laws, conventions and norms of behaviour must not be such that individual creativity is blocked. At the same time, abandoning all laws and values would create complete disorder and social disintegration, as in times of revolution or civil war (see Artigiani, 1987), and at other times when society goes through periods of considerable change so that 'functional paradigms can rapidly become dysfunctional' (Davidson and Rees-Mogg, 1993, p.253). For example, this can occur at a time of rapid technological change which renders existing institutions and values redundant, such as during the industrial revolution (Day, 1993). Arguably the current information-communication revolution threatens to produce another 'phase transition' in social and economic development, equally as unpredictable in its outcome as the arrival of the steam engine.

The current increase in drug abuse and the decline of law and order, especially in inner cities, are relevant, for these trends may reflect a change in social norms away from social stability towards, potentially, explosive instability. Certainly, cultural values have been identified as important factors in the rapid economic development of parts of South-East Asia where there is tighter social cohesion than typically now exists in Europe and North America (for example, see Okimoto, 1989, on the importance of cultural factors in Japanese economic success). Economies with excessive conflict (explosive instability) and those where a shared culture stifles individual creativity (stability leading to ossification) are equally likely to decline. Orthodoxy and the subversion of orthodoxy both need to exist but in a balance. In terms of social policy, governments should pursue that balance. They should avoid policies and expenditures that might produce either growing social instability or excessive social stagnation.

In practice, human intervention in natural systems to dampen fluctuations or remove stresses has often led to perverse results. To take one example: for many years governments attempted to prevent forest fires in US national parks through strict regulations and controls. Unfortunately, it was not appreciated at the time that nature has its own fire fighter. In nature, small forest fires reduce the chance of a bigger and more catastrophic event. By preventing such small fires, the national park authorities unwittingly raised the chances of a devastating inferno. This lesson has now been learned, although it came too late to save the Yellowstone Park from a major fire in 1988 (Jeffery, 1989; Zimmerman and Hurst, 1992, p.10). The moral of the story is that it may be natural to seek sanctuary from the anxiety and uncertainty inherent in life. But in a chaotic world, change and its consequences cannot be avoided – nor should they be.

Economics as Equilibrium: Neo-classical Economics

Recognition that chaotic dynamics are possible and perhaps likely in economies has important implications for the study of economics as well as for economic policy. The dominant paradigm in economics has for long been neo-classical theory. It is difficult, however, to reconcile neo-classical economics with chaos.

Neo-classical economics is broadly concerned with given means and known alternative ends. In its theorising, economic agents are assumed to be rational and to maximise utility, including profits. Information problems are absent or easily defined. In this world, once a market equilibrium is disturbed prices quickly, smoothly and predictably change until demand and supply are back in balance. Unlike dissipative structures, which while retaining their essence are constantly evolving, neo-classical market models are static and conservative. Market movements depend upon negative feedback or built-in dampening mechanisms that respond to internal or external changes. Given a shock, for example, a change in the price of a competitor's product, the market responds to restore a new equilibrium. This equilibrium is stable until another shock comes along.

Uncertainty about means and ends can be handled by neo-classical models, but only where the pattern of outcomes over a whole population of events is known in a probability sense or at least can be conceptually determined (Buchanan and Pierro, 1980, p.693; Stiglitz, 1985). Probability estimation requires that an event is repeated (for instance, a coin is tossed a number of times) or that there is a large number of the same kinds of events. For predictive purposes, it also requires that the underlying relationship will continue to hold into the future. If the event is unique or if the underlying relationship either does not hold or is not known, there can be no probability measure.

Chaotic Dynamics Emphasise Uncertainty

The study of chaotic dynamics draws attention to uncertainty. What is at stake is therefore much more than simple risk. In this world, useful probability measures cannot be attached to uncertain events since true uncertainty implies no knowledge of either future problems or their possible solution.

To take one important example. The neo-classical general equilibrium model, which lies at the heart of neo-classical theorising, involves clearing all markets, including futures markets, simultaneously (Hicks, 1957; Debreu, 1959). Given the existence of an efficient futures market, it is regularly demonstrated to students of economics that supply and demand adjustments can lead to an equilibrium state where future investments are neither over- nor under-subscribed. However, futures markets cannot so function if individuals are unable to ascribe a meaningful probability to future events, which must be so in a chaotic world with its inherent unpredictability. In a chaotic world, futures markets will not adjust to create a 'general equilibrium'. As Kenneth Boulding (1987, p.115) observes: 'Equilibrium is a figment of the human imagination and stability is largely the result of a defect of our time perception.'[6]

The Market as a Process: Austrian Economics

An approach to economics that is more compatible with a world of chaotic dynamics is Austrian economics. Austrian economics is an economic tradition that developed in parallel with neo-classical theory and which shares some of its principles, but which diverged from neo-classical economics during the 20th century. The basis of Austrian economics is 'methodological subjectivism' – that is, individuals are assumed to act purposefully to achieve their desired ends. The economy is therefore understood in terms of the actions and choices of individuals. Individuals operate, however, in a world of imperfect information. In consequence, Austrians believe there are few statistical regularities to make economics a predictive 'science'. At best, economic theories are only qualitative guides to cause and effect. This view is noticeably close to the conclusions from chaos theory regarding unpredictability and irregular patterns of economic behaviour.

Originating, as the name suggests, in the work of Austrian economists (notably Carl Menger (1840-1921), Friedrich von Wieser (1851-1926), Eugen von Böhm-Bawerk (1851-1914), Ludwig von Mises (1881-1973) and Joseph Schumpeter (1883-1950)), today the term 'Austrian' represents a school of thought rather than a geographic tradition. The common theme is a concern with competition as a dynamic and on-going *process* of change (for a very useful review, see Littlechild, 1986). Notable contributions in recent years have come from F.A. Hayek, Israel Kirzner and G.L.S. Shackle. In

---

6 The term 'equilibrium' in economics is used to mean a state of rest or steady state. It is also used to mean a situation where a set of conditions is satisfied. Bullard and Butler (1993) try to salvage the concept of equilibrium in a chaotic world by arguing that equilibrium conditions, such as market clearing, are met even though the dynamic behaviour of the economy is chaotic. They write: 'It may well be that a non-linear world which never converges to a steady state nevertheless has equilibrium paths characterised by perfect competition, perfect foresight, and continuous market clearing' (p.855). It is difficult, however, to see the practical relevance of this statement since perfect foresight cannot exist in a chaotic world – a point they acknowledge later in their paper (p.857).

Hayek's and Kirzner's writings the market is a 'discovery procedure' of ends and means. Information is channelled between potential customers and potential suppliers by prices (Hayek, 1935, 1948, 1978; Kirzner, 1973). In the market economy, entrepreneurial alertness to profit opportunities is crucial in co-ordinating demand and supply. Shackle (1961, 1972) emphasises the problem of gathering and processing information and the rôle of uncertainty when making choices.

In the Austrian approach to economics, change does not disturb what is otherwise an economic equilibrium, as in neo-classical theory. Nor is the central concern with optimal equilibrium solutions. Instead, change is inherent in economic life. Moreover, there can be no guarantee that individuals' responses to change will be optimal in the neo-classical sense. In Austrian thinking, economies move predictably to equilibrium only if information is perfect or complete. Only then will all individual acts be co-ordinated, leading very quickly to no surpluses or deficits in markets (Hayek, 1942, p.290).

In practice, in economics information is not complete and actions are not perfectly co-ordinated, so surpluses and deficits can exist for some time. In this world the function of the market is to act as both an information producer and information processor. Market prices highlight where surpluses and deficits in the economy occur and therefore where there are opportunities to make profits (Cordato, 1980). It is because there is no guarantee that markets will adjust perfectly and instantaneously that enterprise and profit-making are both possible and necessary.

The Neglect of Enterprise and Profit-Making

In neo-classical economics there is little or no scope for entrepreneurial action. Consequently, enterprise and profit-making are neglected subjects in economics textbooks. This explains why, tragically for economic policy-making, generations of economists leave our universities with hardly any understanding of their importance in a market economy (Parker and Stead, 1991). Technical progress and innovation appear to fall like 'manna from heaven' in neo-classical economics. With perfect information about optimal prices, outputs and factor input combinations, there are no entrepreneurial decisions to make.

By contrast, Austrian economics correctly identifies enterprise as being at the heart of the market economy. The entrepreneur acts both as a destabilising force, through innovation in the form of new products and technologies that disrupt existing markets, and as a reactor to the arbitrage opportunities that are consequently created. Schumpeter realised that in the neo-classical world, innovation would not occur because new ideas would be shared. There would be no scope even to make short-term economic rents; if high profits cannot be made, why bother to innovate?

Like Austrian economics, the new science of complexity provides a rationale for enterprise that is missing in a world of equilibria and predictability. In Chapter III we explored the meaning of chaos theory for the management of organisations. We saw that organisations must be continuously adapting to unforeseeable changes in market conditions. In other words, they have to cultivate entrepreneurial activity in order to seek out new opportunities and innovate. The same is true on the larger canvas that is the economy. It is entrepreneurs who provide the continuing energy that the economy, as a dissipative system, requires. In providing this input the entrepreneur is more than a risk-taker. Risk involves a probability of success or failure. As Frank Knight observed many years ago:

'Situations in regard to which business judgement must be exercised do not repeat themselves with sufficient conformity to type to make possible a computation of probability' (Knight, 1951, p.120).

Entrepreneurial choice is not informed by formal theories of probability. In complex and imperfectly understood market conditions, entrepreneurship is much more a matter of hunch than of computed, expected values.

Austrian economists view the future as indeterminate, while chaotic dynamics identifies it as determinate but so complex as to be unpredictable. In practice, we cannot identify and measure all of the necessary variables which will determine the precise future. For policy purposes, both views amount to the same thing. If the variables which determine the future cannot be identified or measured, even in probabilistic terms, then they cannot be managed or planned. Austrian economics, unlike neo-classical theory, complements a world of chaotic dynamics. Indeed, an appreciation of chaos in economic relationships adds strength to the Austrian rejection of a knowable future. Moreover, Austrian economists have been long-time critics of macro-economic forecasting and of state planning and demand management.

Chaos and the Study of Economics

Chaos theory adds an important dimension to the study of economics. It helps to explain why economies are subject to aperiodic and unheralded turbulence. It also helps to explain why economies are so difficult to forecast and plan. Indeed, as we have seen, forecasting is a highly questionable activity; while attempting to plan the long-term future of an economy seems futile. Instead, policy should be aimed at providing the right environment for stability within instability, leading to creative change.

An economic system is required which encourages adaptability without provoking explosive instability – an economy that encourages the production of information so that economic agents adapt quickly and as smoothly as possible to economic changes. In other words, it requires an economic system that places a premium on flexibility and innovation. A competitive economy that encourages enterprise and the process of change is best able to contend with the unknowable, chaotic future.

V. CONCLUSIONS AND POLICY RECOMMENDATIONS

'We are in the nature of things in some respects blind....'

(G.L.S. Shackle, 1988, p.x)

Chaos theory was first explored in the natural sciences. But the purpose of this *Hobart Paper* is to highlight its relevance to the study of business and economics. The main theme is that, as in nature, firms and economies have important non-linear feedback loops which cause them to operate far from equilibrium, where small and seemingly insignificant disturbances become strongly amplified. It is when systems operate far from equilibrium that they are inherently creative.

The implications of this finding for our understanding of the way firms and economies behave are profound. Recognition of the importance of chaotic dynamics to the study of management and the economy can initially be uncomfortable. Old forms of reasoning have to be abandoned and a new form of thinking adopted. But to understand how businesses and economies actually operate, this transformation cannot be avoided.

This *Paper* has explained the nature of bounded instability or chaos, drawing attention to the main features of chaotic dynamics in systems. It has also explored the implications for firms at the strategic management level and for economic planning, especially macro-economic planning, allowing a new perspective on the rôle of markets.

More specifically, the analysis points to the following conclusions and policy recommendations:

O In a chaotic world, the longer-term economic future is inherently unknowable. It cannot be predicted or usefully planned except in the most general terms. Hence, at both the firm and macro-economic levels, policy should aim to provide conditions which allow economic agents to adapt and create. Competitive markets have an important rôle to play in this process. Unlike planned systems, they provide for spontaneous adaptation.

O Research in the physical sciences demonstrates that, to be innovative, a system must operate at the chaos frontier. Here links between actions and long-term outcomes are lost in the detail of the interaction. The same is true of social and economic systems. Agents within an economic system choose their next action, but they cannot choose its long-term outcome. Choice is therefore real. The long-term outcome is not predetermined by some given state of a future environment. Chaos permits true choice in economic systems.

O Enterprise is a locomotive of change in competitive market economies. By drawing attention to the importance of adaptability and change, chaos theory provides a new argument for the innovating entrepreneur. Only in systems where there is real choice can there be the unique behaviour implicit in the act of enterprise. Economies which cope best with chaotic conditions are likely to be those which promote entrepreneurial adaptation.

O Chaos theory may help to explain why economies are subject to turbulence. The creative market economy will not be stable, even in the absence of exogenous shocks. Equally, however, there seems no conceivable way in which state intervention can guarantee to reduce economic fluctuations. Indeed, slight errors in demand management may be highly magnified, leading to even greater economic instability. Governments add to uncertainty by frequent and unpredicted changes in regulations, public spending and taxation.

O Any system which attempts conscious design or planning of long-term futures will inevitably break down. Companies and economies require structures and institutions which encourage self-transformation. In terms of policy we should be focussing on means rather than ends, creating the conditions for change by designing systems that are capable of self-organising evolution.

[93]

O Both the traditional ('rational') management literature and neo-classical economics have real problems in handling change where longer-term consequences are inherently unpredictable and even, perhaps, unimaginable. The economics profession, in particular, trained in neo-classical model building, has created an aura of scientific competence which seems entirely misplaced. It is difficult to justify the neo-classical preoccupation with equilibrium states involving amplitude-reducing, negative-feedback relationships.

O Neo-classical economics removes the dynamics of an economic system by making the world essentially known or at least knowable. The conclusions of chaos theory are more compatible with the methodology and policy prescriptions of Austrian economics with its themes of spontaneous self-organisation, enterprise and creative destruction. In Austrian economics, social and economic evolution take place in the context of a non-equilibrium world, in which economic agents rarely achieve their plans exactly, and the emphasis is on economic *processes*, not existing states or structures.

O Chaos theory suggests that the world is best understood as one in which firms and hence economies evolve along complex time trajectories, which are beyond our ability fully to understand. Firms and economies which are best able to succeed are, therefore, those which are open to change and at the same time can contain the resulting social and economic tensions. Achieving this 'creative tension' or order within disorder requires both institutions and behavioural norms that promote adaptability. In particular, government economic and social policy should complement not conflict with economic change. This raises questions about policies that *reduce* the economy's ability to adapt, including regulation, monopoly and high taxation, insofar as they diminish the willingness or ability of economic agents to innovate or change their behaviour. A similar point may apply to welfare policies and government expenditures. Policies towards government taxation and expenditure entail a delicate balance. For example, high levels of taxation are likely to reduce the economy's flexibility. At the same time, they may be thought necessary to fund welfare programmes that prevent social unrest or which are judged to be in some sense ethically imperative.

O Economic relations emerge from and are bounded by cultural and social behaviour as well as laws. When these social norms begin to break down or change dramatically, there will be an unpredictable interrelationship with economic change. More understanding of this inter-relationship is required, and especially its positive, destabilising, feedback effects. We also need to know more about the impact of state policies on this process. In the early post-war decades there was prosperity and relatively little social and economic turbulence in Europe and North America. But since the 1960s there has apparently been increased turbulence, both social and economic. This development is difficult to explain in terms of equilibrium systems, but chaos theory may provide a route to the answer.

The study of chaotic dynamics requires managers, economists and policy-makers to re-assess many existing views about how economic agents function. It requires them to undertake the sort of double-loop learning which is necessary when an existing mental model of the world is no longer appropriate. An appreciation of chaotic dynamics prompts questions about and changes in the existing shared mental model of economic relationships.

To sum up, this *Hobart Paper* suggests that chaos theory from the natural sciences provides a new and exciting departure point for the study of organisations and economies. However, like all departures to an unknown future we cannot begin to imagine the details of the journey. Nor can we determine where it will eventually lead.

GLOSSARY

Adaptive Fit
A term which describes a strategy concerned with developing and maintaining a viable match between the opportunities and threats outside the organisation and the organisation's capabilities and resources.

Attractor
An attractor binds a system to a pattern of behaviour. This may be attraction to a stable point, to a regular cycle or to more complex forms of behaviour (*q.v.* **Strange Attractor** below)

Bounded Instability
A system which is boundedly unstable has complex oscillations but not completely unstable behaviour. There are limits to the instability.

Chaotic Turbulence
Occurs when the behaviour of a system is subject to unstable oscillations.

Dissipative Structures
Contain forces due to friction that dissipate energy, but they still preserve a structure. Dissipative structures can evolve, sometimes in unexpected and sudden ways.

Endogenous Turbulence
Turbulence in behaviour which occurs not because of outside influences or shocks. It is coded into the behaviour of the system.

Fractal
A fractal shape is one made up of parts which are self similar. This means that the shape is made up of parts which are similar in structure to the shape itself. Each of those parts is in turn made up of similar parts on a smaller scale, and so on

into an infinite regress. As might be imagined, the mathematics of such objects is complex.

Long-Range Coherence
Behaviour which is ordered across the whole system.

Phase Transition
A sudden qualitative change in a system's behaviour.

Sensitive Dependence (on Initial Conditions)
An important feature of the disorderly behaviour of deterministic dynamic systems in science. In particular, it is responsible for their unpredictability, for the system can be sensitive even to minute changes in the value of its conditions or parameters. Very small variations in parameter values lead to great variations in behaviour of the system.

Strange Attractor
An attractor which has multiple points of attraction within a finite space. Where the attractor is strange the system's behaviour becomes unstable but within bounds (*q.v.* **Bounded Instability** above).

Stochastic Shocks (or Effects)
Random external shocks or disturbances.

TOPICS/QUESTIONS FOR DISCUSSION

1. What are the general implications of non-linear dynamics for the study of firms and economies?

2. Why might it be dangerous to adopt a linear approximation of a non-linear system?

3. Why in a chaotic world is the longer-term future inherently unknowable?

4. In what ways is it useful to view firms and economies as dissipative systems?

5. What is meant by the notion that economic systems, to be changeable, must operate far from equilibrium?

6. Why do managers and policy-makers so often fail to realise the outcomes they intend?

7. In what ways is the traditional literature with its 'rational' approach to management and economic policy-making deficient?

8. Any system which we consciously try to design or plan over the longer term will inevitably break down. Why?

9. Why does chaos theory confront the neo-classical paradigm but complement Austrian economics?

10. In what ways does chaos theory provide a new argument for entrepreneurship?

REFERENCES/BIBLIOGRAPHY

Anzieu, D. (1984): *The Group and the Unconscious*, London: Routledge & Kegan Paul.

Argyris, C. (1990): *Overcoming Organizational Defenses: Facilitating Organizational Learning*, Boston, Mass.: Allyn & Bacon, Prentice Hall.

Argyris, C., and D. Schön (1978): *Organizational Learning: a Theory of Action Perspective*, Reading, Mass.: Addison Wesley.

Arthur, W.B. (1989): 'Competing Technologies, Increasing Returns, and Lock-In by Historical Events', *Economic Journal*, Vol.99, March, pp.116-31.

Arthur, W.B. (1990): 'Positive Feedbacks in the Economy', *Scientific American*, February, pp.80-85.

Artigiani, R. (1987): 'Organizing the Nation: Revolution and the State', *European Journal of Operational Research*, Vol.30, pp.208-10.

Barnett, W., and P. Chen (1986): *Deterministic Chaos and Fractal Attractors as Tools of Nonparametric Dynamical Econometric Inference with an Application to the Divisia Monetary Aggregates*, Technical Report No.33, Centre for Statistical Studies, Austin: University of Texas.

Baumol, W.J. (1968): 'Entrepreneurship in Economic Theory', *American Economic Review*, Vol.58, May, pp.64-71.

Baumol, W.J. (1987): 'The Chaos Phenomenon: a Nightmare for Forecasters', *LSE Quarterly*, No.1, Spring, pp.99-114.

Baumol, W.J., and J. Benhabib (1989): 'Chaos: Significance, Mechanism, and Economic Applications', *Journal of Economic Perspectives*, Vol.3, No.1, Winter, pp.77-105.

Baumol, W.J., and E.N. Wolff (1983): 'Feedback from Productivity Growth to R&D', *Scandinavian Journal of Economics*, Vol.85, No.2, pp.147-57.

Baumol, W.J., and R.E. Quandt (1985): 'Chaos Models and their Implications for Forecasting', *Eastern Economic Journal*, Vol.11, No.1, pp.3-15.

[99]

Beck, P. (1981): *Corporate Plans for an Uncertain Future*, London: Shell UK.

Beer, M., R.A. Eisenstat, and B. Spector (1990): *The Critical Path to Corporate Renewal*, Boston, Mass.: Harvard Business School Press.

Benhabib, J., and R.H. Day (1980): 'Erratic Accumulation', *Economic Letters*, Vol.6, No.1, pp.113-17.

Benhabib, J., and R.H. Day (1982): 'A Characterization of Erratic Dynamics in the Overlapping Generations Model', *Journal of Economic Dynamics and Control*, Vol.4, No.1, pp.37-55.

Berge, P., Y. Pomeau, and C. Vidal (1984): *Order within Chaos*, New York: Wiley.

Bion, W.R. (1961): *Experiences in Groups and Other Papers*, London: Tavistock Publications.

Boldrin, M., and M. Woodford (1990): 'Equilibrium Models Displaying Endogenous Fluctuations and Chaos: a Survey', *Journal of Monetary Economics*, Vol.25, March, pp.189-223.

Boulding, K.E. (1981): *Evolutionary Economics*, Beverly Hills, CA: Sage.

Boulding, K.E. (1987): 'The Epistemology of Complexity', *European Journal of Operational Research*, Vol.30, pp.110-16.

Briggs, J., and F.D. Peat (1989): *Turbulent Mirror*, New York: Harper and Row.

Brock, W.A. (1988): *Overlapping Generations Models with Money and Transactions Costs*, Department of Economics Workshop series, SSRI No.8815, University of Wisconsin-Madison.

Brock, W.A., and C.L. Sayers (1988): 'Is the Business Cycle Characterized by Deterministic Chaos?', *Journal of Monetary Economics*, Vol.22, No.1, pp.71-90.

Brock, W.A., and A. Malliaris (1989): *Differential Equations, Stability and Chaos in Dynamic Economics*, Amsterdam: North-Holland.

Buchanan, J.M., and A. di Pierro (1980): 'Cognition, Choice, and Entrepreneurship', *Southern Economic Journal*, Vol.46, pp.693-701.

Bullard, J., and A. Butler (1993): 'Nonlinearity and Chaos in Economic Models: Implications for Policy Decisions', *Economic Journal*, Vol.103, July, pp.849-67.

Burgess, S.M. (1993): 'Nonlinear Dynamics in a Structural Model of Employment', in M.H. Pesaran and S.M. Potter (eds.), *Nonlinear Dynamics, Chaos and Econometrics*, Chichester, Sussex: John Wiley.

Cao, C.Q., and R.S. Tsay (1993): 'Nonlinear Time-Series Analysis of Stock Volatilities', in Pesaran and Potter (eds.).

Cartwright, T.J. (1991): 'Planning and Chaos Theory', *Journal of the American Planning Association*, Vol.57, Winter, pp.44-56.

Casson, M. (1991): *The Economics of Business Culture*, Oxford: Clarendon Press.

Chen, P. (1988): 'Empirical and Theoretical Evidence of Economic Chaos', *System Dynamics Review*, Vol.4, Nos.1-2, pp.81-108.

Cordato, R.E. (1980): 'The Austrian Theory of Efficiency and the Role of Government', *The Journal of Libertarian Studies*, Vol.4, No.4, Fall, pp.393-403.

Cowen, T., and J. Ellig (1993): *Koch Industries and Market-Based Management*, Working Paper in Market-Based Management, Fairfax, VA.: George Mason University.

Cunningham, S.R. (1989): *Monetary Equilibria and Chaos* (PhD Thesis), The Florida State University.

Dana, R.A., and P. Malgrange (1984): 'The Dynamics of a Discrete Version of a Growth Cycle Model', in J.P. Ancot (ed.), *Analyzing the Structure of Econometric Models*, Amsterdam: M. Nighoff.

Davidson, J.D., and W. Rees-Mogg (1993): *The Great Reckoning: How the World Will Change in the Depression of the 1990s*, revised edition, London: Sidgwick & Jackson.

Day, R.H. (1982): 'Irregular Growth Cycles', *American Economic Review*, Vol.72, No.3, pp.406-14.

Day, R.H. (1983): 'The Emergence of Chaos from Classical Economic Growth', *Quarterly Journal of Economics*, Vol.98, pp.201-13.

Day, R.H., and W. Shafer (1985): 'Keynesian Chaos', *Journal of Macroeconomics*, Vol.7, No.3, pp.277-95.

Day, R.H., and J.L. Walter (1989): 'Economic Growth in the Very Long-Run: or the Multiple Phase Interaction of Population, Technology and Social Infrastructure', in W. Barnett, J. Geweke, and K. Shells (eds.), *Economic Complexity: Chaos, Sunspots, Bubbles and Nonlinearity*, Cambridge, Mass.: Cambridge University Press.

[101]

Day, R.H. (1993): 'Complex Economic Dynamics: Obvious in History, Generic in Theory, Elusive in Data', in Pesaran and Potter (eds.).

De Coster, G., and D. Mitchell (1991): 'Nonlinear Monetary Dynamics', *Journal of Business and Economic Statistics*, Vol.9, No.4, pp.455-61.

De Geus, A.P. (1988): 'Planning as Learning', *Harvard Business Review*, March-April, pp.70-74.

Debreu, G. (1959): *Theory of Value*, New Haven, CT: Yale University Press.

Deneckere, R., and K.L. Judd (1986): *Cyclical and Chaotic Behavior in a Dynamic Equilibrium Model with Implications for Fiscal Policy*, CMSEMS, Discussion Paper No.734, Evanston, IL: Northwestern University.

Dow, J.C.R. (1970): *The Management of the British Economy 1945-60*, Cambridge, Mass.: Cambridge University Press.

Doz, Y.L., and C.K. Prahalad (1991): 'Managing DMNCs: a Search for a new Paradigm', *Strategic Management Journal*, Vol.12, pp.145-64.

Dumaine, B. (1991): 'The Bureaucracy Busters', *Fortune*, 17 June, pp.36-50.

Economist, The (1993): 'A Survey of the Frontiers of Finance', 9 October.

Ellig, J. (1993): *Internal Pricing for Corporate Services*, Working Paper in Market-Based Management, Fairfax, VA.: George Mason University.

Feigenbaum, M.J.(1978): 'Quantitative Universality for a Class of Nonlinear Transformations', *Journal of Statistical Physics*, Vol.19, No.1, pp.25-52.

Fine, G. (1984): 'Negotiated Order and Organizational Cultures', *Annual Review of Sociology*, Vol.10, pp.2,239-62.

Forrester, J.W. (1958): 'Industrial Dynamics: a Major Breakthrough for Decision Making', *Harvard Business Review*, Vol.36, No.4, pp.37-66.

Forrester, J.W. (1961): *Industrial Dynamics*, Cambridge, Mass.: MIT Press.

Frank, M., R. Gencay, and T. Stengos (1988): 'International Chaos', *European Economic Review*, Vol.32, No.8, pp.1,568-84.

Frank, M., and T. Stengos (1987): *Measuring the Strangeness of Gold and Silver Rates of Return*, Department of Economics Discussion Paper No.1986-13, Ontario, Canada: University of Guelph.

Frank, M., and T. Stengos (1988a): 'Chaotic Dynamics in Economic Time-Series', *Journal of Economic Surveys*, Vol.2, No.2, pp.103-33.

Frank, M., and T. Stengos (1988b): 'Some Evidence Concerning Macroeconomic Chaos', *Journal of Monetary Economics*, Vol.22, pp.423-38.

Frank, M., and T. Stengos (1989): *Nearest Neighbor Forecasts of Precious Metals Rates of Return*, Department of Economics Discussion Paper No.1989-2, Ontario, Canada: University of Guelph.

Frisch, R. (1933): *Propagation Problems and Impulse Problems in Dynamic Economics: Economic Essays in Honour of Gustav Cassel*, London: George Allen and Unwin.

Gabisch, G., and H.W. Lorenz (1989): *Business Cycle Theory: a Survey of Methods and Concepts*, Berlin: Springer-Verlag.

Gable, W., and J. Ellig (1993): *Introduction to Market-Based Management*, Fairfax, VA.: Centre for the Study of Market Processes.

Gleick, J. (1987): *Chaos: Making a New Science*, London: Penguin Books.

Goodwin, R.M. (1986): 'The Economy as an Evolutionary Pulsator', *Journal of Economic Behavior and Organization*, Vol.7, No.4, pp.341-49.

Grandmont, J.M. (1985): 'On Endogenous Competitive Business Cycles', *Econometrica*, Vol.53, pp.995-1,045.

Grandmont, J.M. (1986): 'Stabilizing Competitive Business Cycles', *Journal of Economic Theory*, Vol.40, No.1, pp.57-76.

Grandmont, J.M. (1989): 'Keynesian Issues and Economic Theory', *Scandinavian Journal of Economics*, Vol.91, No.2, pp.265-94.

Halal, W.E. (1986): *The New Capitalism*, New York: John Wiley.

Halal, W.E., A. Geranmayeh, and J. Proudehnad (1993): *Internal Markets: Bringing the Power of Free Enterprise inside the Organisation*, New York: John Wiley.

Haldane, J.B.S. (1928): *Possible Worlds and Other Essays*, London: Chatto & Windus.

[103]

Hammer, M., and J. Champy (1993): *Reengineering the Corporation: a Manifesto for Business Revolution*, London: Nicholas Brealey.

Hampden-Turner, C. (1990): *Charting the Corporate Mind*, New York: Free Press.

Handy, C. (1994): *The Empty Raincoat: Making Sense of the Future*, London: Hutchinson.

Hanna, D.P. (1988): *Designing Organizations for High Performance*, Reading, Mass.: Addison Wesley.

Hayek, F.A. (1935): *Collectivist Economic Planning*, London: Routledge & Kegan Paul.

Hayek, F.A. (1942): 'Scientism and the Study of Society', *Economica*, Vol.9, August, pp.267-91.

Hayek, F.A. (1948): *Individualism and Economic Order*, Chicago: University of Chicago Press.

Hayek, F.A. (1978): *New Studies in Philosophy, Politics and Economics and the History of Ideas*, London: Routledge and Kegan Paul.

Hicks, J.R. (1957): *Value and Capital*, London: Oxford University Press.

Hirschhorn, L. (1990): *The Workplace Within: Psychodynamics of Organizational Life*, Cambridge, Mass.: MIT Press.

Hodgson, G.M. (1988): *Economics and Institutions: A Manifesto for a Modern Institutional Economics*, Cambridge: Polity Press.

Howard, R. (ed.) (1993): *The Learning Imperative: Managing People for Continuous Innovation*, Boston, Mass.: Harvard Business School Press.

Hsieh, D.A. (1989): 'Testing for Nonlinear Dependence in Daily Foreign Exchange Rates', *Journal of Business*, Vol.62, pp.339-67.

Hsieh, D.A. (1991): 'Chaos and Nonlinear Dynamics: Application to Financial Markets', *Journal of Finance*, Vol.46, No.5, pp.1,839-77.

Invernizzi, S., and A. Medio (1991): 'On Lags and Chaos in Economic Dynamic Models', *Journal of Mathematical Economics*, Vol.20, pp.521-50.

Jacques, E. (1955): 'Social Systems as a Defence against Persecutory and Defensive Anxiety', in P. Heimann and P. Money-Kyrle (eds.), *New Directions in Psychoanalysis*, London: Tavistock Publications. Also published in G.S. Gibbard, J.J. Hartman, and

R.D. Mann (eds.) (1974): *Analysis of Groups*, San Francisco: Jossey-Bass.

Jantsch, E. (1980): *The Self-Organizing Universe*, Oxford: Pergamon Press.

Jeffery, D. (1989): 'Yellowstone: Fires of 1988', *National Geographic*, Vol.175, No.2, pp.255-73.

Johannisson, B. (1993): 'Organisational Networks and Innovations', in R. Stacey (ed.), *Strategic Thinking and the Management of Change: International Perspectives on Organisational Dynamics*, London: Kogan Page.

Johnson, G. (1987): *Strategic Change and Management Process*, Oxford: Blackwell.

Johnson, G. (1988): 'Rethinking Incrementalism', *Strategic Management Journal*, Vol.9, pp.75-91.

Kamminga, H. (1990): 'What is this thing called chaos?', *New Left Review*, No.181, May/June, pp.49-59.

Kay, J. (1993): *The Foundations of Corporate Success: How Business Strategies Add Value*, Oxford: Oxford University Press.

Kelsey, D. (1988): 'The Economics of Chaos or the Chaos of Economics', *Oxford Economic Papers*, Vol.40, No.1, March, pp.1-31.

Kirzner, I.M. (1973): *Competition and Entrepreneurship*, Chicago: University of Chicago Press.

Kirzner, I.M. (1976): 'On the Method of Austrian Economics', in E.G. Dolan (ed.), *The Foundations of Modern Austrian Economics*, Kansas City: Sheed and Ward.

Kirzner, I.M. (1985): *Discovery and the Capitalist Process*, Chicago: University of Chicago Press.

Knight, F.H. (1951): *The Economic Organization*, New York: Augustus M. Kelley.

Kolmogorov, A.N. (1941): 'Local Structure of Turbulence in an Incompressible Liquid for Very Large Rayleigh Numbers', *Doklady Akademii Nauk, USSR*, Vol.30, No.2, pp.299-303.

Krugman, P. (1991): 'Target Zones and Exchange Rate Dynamics', *Quarterly Journal of Economics*, Vol.106, pp.669-82.

Lacity, M.C., and R. Hirshheim (1993): *Information Systems Outsourcing: Myths, Metaphors and Reality*, Chichester, Sussex: John Wiley.

Leslie, T.E.C. (1879): *Essays in Political and Moral Philosophy*, Dublin: Hodges, Foster and Figgis.

Littlechild, S.C. (1986): *The Fallacy of the Mixed Economy: an 'Austrian' critique of recent economic thinking and policy*, Hobart Paper No.80, Second Edn., London: Institute of Economic Affairs.

Loasby, B.J. (1976): *Choice, Complexity, and Ignorance: an Enquiry into Economic Theory and Practice of Decision Making*, Cambridge: Cambridge University Press.

Loasby, B.J. (1982): 'The Entrepreneur in Economic Theory', *Scottish Journal of Political Economy*, Vol.29, No.3, November, pp.235-45.

Lorenz, E. (1963): 'Deterministic Nonperiodic Flow', *Journal of the Atmospheric Sciences*, Vol.20, No.2, March, pp.130-41.

Loye, D., and R. Eisler (1987): 'Chaos and Transformation: Implications of Nonequilibrium Theory for Social Science and Society', *Behavioral Science*, Vol.32, January, pp.53-65.

Lucas, R.E., Jr. (1975): 'An Equilibrium Model of the Business Cycle', *Journal of Political Economy*, Vol.83, pp.985-92.

Lucas, R.E., Jr. (1981): *Studies in Business Cycle Theory*, Cambridge, Mass.: MIT Press.

Lyapunov, A.M. (1892, republished 1950): *Obshchaya Zadacha ob Restoichivisti Dvizheniya (The General Stability of Motion)*, Moscow-Leningrad: Gosteklhizdat.

Malabre, A.L., Jr. (1993): *Lost Prophets*, Boston, Mass.: Harvard Business School Press.

Malthus, T.R. (1817): *An Essay on the Principle of Population as it Affects the Future Improvement of Society* (5th edn., 19?), Homewood, Ill.: Richard D.Irwin.

Mandelbrot, B. (1977): *The Fractal Geometry of Nature*, New York: Freeman.

McCaffrey, D., S. Ellner, A. Gallant, and D. Nychka (1992): 'Estimating the Lyapunov Exponent of a Chaotic System with Nonparametric Regression', *Journal of the American Statistical Association*, Vol.87, No.419, pp.682-95.

Medio, A. (1991): 'Continuous-Time Models of Chaos in Economics', *Journal of Economic Behavior & Organization*, Vol.16, July, pp.115-51.

Medio, A. (in collaboration with G. Gallo) (1992): *Chaotic Dynamics: Theory and Applications to Economics*, Cambridge: Cambridge University Press.

Menzies, I. (1975): 'A Case Study in the Functioning of Social Systems as a Defence against Anxiety', in A. Coleman and W.H. Bexton (eds.), *Group Relations Reader*, Sausalito, California: Grex.

Meyerson, D., and J. Martin (1987): 'Cultural Change: an Integration of Three Different Views', *Journal of Management Studies*, Vol.24, pp.623-47.

Miller, D., and P.H. Friesen (1980): 'Momentum and Revolution in Organizational Adaptation', *Academy of Management Journal*, Vol.23, pp.591-614.

Miller, D., and K. de Vries (1987): *The Neurotic Organization*, San Francisco: Jossey Bass.

Miller, D. (1990): *The Icarus Paradox: How Excellent Organisations Can Bring about their own Downfall*, New York: Harper Business.

Miller, E. (1993): 'The Human Dynamic', in R. Stacey (ed.), *Strategic Thinking and the Management of Change: International Perspectives on Organisational Dynamics*, London: Kogan Page.

Mintzberg, H. (1994): *The Rise and Fall of Strategic Planning*, London: Prentice Hall.

Mitchell, W.C. (1988): *Government As It Is*, Hobart Paper No.109, London: Institute of Economic Affairs.

Mokey, B.W. (1988): *Entrepreneurship and Public Policy: Can Government Stimulate Business Startups?*, Westport, Conn.: Quorum Books.

Morgan, G. (1993): *Imaginization: the Art of Creative Management*, London: Sage.

Nohria, N., and R.G. Eccles (1993): *Networks and Organizations: Structure, Form and Action*, Boston, Mass.: Harvard Business School Press.

Nonaka, I. (1988): 'Creating Organizational Order Out of Chaos: Self-Renewal in Japanese Firms', *California Management Review*, Spring, pp.57-93.

Odiorne, G.S. (1991): 'Chaos in Management', *Manage*, Vol.43, No.1, pp.4-7.

[107]

Okimoto, D.I. (1989): *Between MITI and the Market: Japanese Industrial Policy for High Technology*, Stanford, Cal.: Stanford University Press.

Park, Y.-B. (1991): *Testing for Chaos in the Foreign Exchange Market*, Working Papers in Commerce, WPC 91/31, Department of Commerce, University of Birmingham.

Parker, D. (1994): 'Privatisation and the International Business Environment', in S. Segal-Horn (ed.), *The Challenge of International Business*, London: Kogan Page.

Parker, D., and R. Stead (1991): *Profit and Enterprise: the Political Economy of Profit*, London: Harvester/Wheatsheaf, and New York: St Martin's Press.

Pascale, R.T. (1990: 1992 edn.): *Managing on the Edge: How Successful Companies Use Conflict to Stay Ahead*, London: Viking Penguin.

Pasour, E.C., Jr. (1978): 'Cost and Choice - Austrian *vs* Conventional Views', *Journal of Libertarian Studies*, Vol.2, No.4, pp.327-36.

Peitgen, H.-O., and P.H. Richter (1986): *The Beauty of Fractals*, Berlin: Springer-Verlag.

Penrose, R. (1989): *The Emperor's New Mind: Concerning Computers, Minds and the Laws of Physics*, Oxford: Oxford University Press.

Perry, L.T., R.G. Stott, and W.N. Smallwood (1993): *Improvising Team-Based Planning for a Fast Changing World*, Chichester, Sussex: John Wiley.

Pesaran, M.H., and S.M. Potter (eds.) (1993): *Nonlinear Dynamics, Chaos and Econometrics*, Chichester, Sussex: John Wiley.

Pesaran, M.H., and S.M. Potter (1993): 'Nonlinear Dynamics, Chaos and Econometrics: an Introduction', in Pesaran and Potter (eds.).

Pesaran, M.H., and H. Samiei (1992): 'Estimating Limited-Dependent Rational Expectations Models with an Application to Exchange Rate Determination in a Target Zone', *Journal of Econometrics*, Vol.53, pp.141-63.

Peters, E.E. (1991): *Chaos and Order in the Capital Markets: a New View of Cycles, Prices and Market Volatility*, New York: John Wiley.

Peters, E.E. (1994): *Fractal Market Analysis*, Chichester, Sussex: John Wiley.

Peters, T. (1987): *Thriving on Chaos: Handbook for a Management Revolution*, London: Macmillan.

Peters, T., and R.H. Waterman (1982): *In Search of Excellence*, New York: Harper and Rowe.

Popper, K.R. (1972): *The Logic of Scientific Discovery*, London: Hutchinson.

Porter, M. (1980): *Competitive Strategy*, New York: Free Press.

Porter, M. (1985): *Competitive Advantage*, New York: Free Press.

Porter, M. (1990): *The Competitive Advantage of Nations*, London: Macmillan.

Prigogine, I. (1980): *From Being to Becoming*, San Francisco: Freeman.

Prigogine, I., and I. Stengers (1984): *Order out of Chaos: Man's New Dialogue with Nature*, New York: Bantam Books.

Prigogine, I. (1988): 'Exploring Complexity', in P.W. Anderson, K.J. Arrow and D. Pines (eds.), *The Economy as a Complex Evolving System: The Proceedings of the Evolutionary Paths of the Global Economy Workshop, September 1987, Santa Fe*, Redwood City, Cal.: Addison-Wesley.

Prokopenko, J., and I. Pavlin (1991): *Entrepreneurship Development in Public Enterprises*, Management Development Series No.29, Geneva: ILO.

Quinn, J.B. (1978): 'Strategic Change: Logical Incrementalism', *Sloan Management Review*, Vol.1, No.20, Fall, pp.7-21.

Quinn, J.B. (1980): *Strategies for Change: Logical Incrementalism*, Homewood, Ill.: Richard D. Irwin.

Rand, D. (1978): 'Exotic Phenomena in Games and Duopoly Models', *Journal of Mathematical Economics*, Vol.5, pp.173-84.

Richards, D. (1990): 'Is Strategic Decision Making Chaotic?', *Behavioral Science*, Vol.35, pp.219-32.

Richardson, G.B. (1963, reprinted 1990): *Information and Investment*, Oxford: Oxford University Press.

Rosser, J.B., Jr. (1990): 'Chaos Theory and the New Keynesian Economics', *The Manchester School*, Vol.58, No.3, pp.265-91.

Ruelle, D., and F. Takens (1971): 'On the Nature of Turbulence', *Communications in Mathematical Physics*, Vol.20, No.3, pp.167-92.

[109]

Samuelson, P. (1939): 'Interactions Between the Multiplier Analysis and the Principle of Acceleration', *Review of Economic Studies*, Vol.21, pp.75-78.

Sayers, C. (1986): *Work Stoppages: Exploring the Nonlinear Dynamics*, Department of Economics working paper, University of Houston.

Senge, P.M. (1990): *The Fifth Discipline: the Art and Practice of the Learning Organization*, New York: Doubleday Currency.

Shackle, G.L.S. (1961): *Decision, Order and Time*, Cambridge: Cambridge University Press.

Shackle, G.L.S. (1972): *Epistemics and Economics*, Cambridge: Cambridge University Press.

Shackle, G.L.S. (1982): 'Means and Meaning in Economic Theory', *Scottish Journal of Political Economy*, Vol.29, No.3, November, pp.223-34.

Shackle, G.L.S. (1983): 'The Bounds of Unknowledge', in J. Wiseman (ed.), *Beyond Positive Economics?*, London: Macmillan.

Scheinkman, J.A. (1990): 'Nonlinearities in Economic Dynamics', *The Economic Journal*, Vol.100, pp.33-48.

Scheinkman, J.A., and B. LeBaron (1987): *Nonlinear Dynamics and GNP Data*, Department of Economics working paper, University of Chicago.

Scheinkman, J.A., and B. LeBaron (1989): 'Nonlinear Dynamics and Stock Returns', *Journal of Business*, Vol.62, No.3, pp.311-37.

Schumpeter, J.A. (1934): *The Theory of Economic Development*, Cambridge, Mass.: Harvard University Press.

Schumpeter, J.A. (1942): *Capitalism, Socialism and Democracy*, New York: Harper.

Schuster, H.G. (1989): *Deterministic Chaos: an Introduction*, New York and Weinheim: VCH.

Schwartz, H.S. (1990): *Narcissistic Process and Organizational Decay: the Theory of the Organizational Ideal*, New York: New York University Press.

Simon, H.A. (1957): *Administrative Behaviour*, New York: Free Press.

Simon, H.A. (1960): *The New Science of Management Decisions*, New York: Harper Brothers.

Smale, S. (1963): 'Diffeomorphisms with many Periodic Points', in S.S. Cairns (ed.), *Differential and Combinatorial Topology*, Princeton, NJ: Princeton University Press.

Smale, S. (1980): *The Mathematics of Time: Essays on Dynamical Systems, Economic Processes and Related Topics*, New York: Springer-Verlag.

Stacey, R. (1991): *The Chaos Frontier: Creative Strategic Control for Business*, Oxford: Butterworth-Heinemann.

Stacey, R. (1992): *Managing the Unknowable : the Strategic Boundaries between Order and Chaos*, San Francisco: Jossey Bass; published in the UK as *Managing Chaos: Dynamic Business Strategies in an Unpredictable World*, London: Kogan Page.

Stacey, R. (1993): *Strategic Management and Organisational Dynamics*, London: Pitman.

Stewart, I. (1989): *Does God Play Dice? The Mathematics of Chaos*, Oxford: Blackwell.

Stiglitz, J.E. (1985): 'Information and Economic Analysis: a Perspective', *Economic Journal*, conference papers, Vol.95, pp.21-41.

Terasvirta, T., and H.M. Anderson (1993): 'Characterising Nonlinearities in Business Cycles using Smooth Transition Autoregressive Models', in Pesaran and Potter (eds.).

Thompson, J.D., and A. Tuden (1959): 'Strategies, Structures and Processes of Organisational Decisions', in J.D. Thompson *et al.* (eds.), *Comparative Studies in Administration*, Pittsburgh: University of Pittsburgh Press.

Thompson, J.D. (1967): *Organizations in Action*, New York: McGraw-Hill.

Town, R.J. (1993): 'Merger Waves and the Structure of Merger and Acquisition Time Series', in Pesaran and Potter (eds.).

Tsoukas, H. (1991): 'The Missing Link: a Transformational View of Metaphors in Organizational Science', *Academy of Management Review*, Vol.16, No.3, pp.566-85.

Wack, P. (1985): 'Scenarios, Shooting the Rapids', *Harvard Business Review*, Nov.-Dec., pp.139-50.

Waldrop, W.M. (1994): *Complexity: the Emerging Science at the Edge of Order and Chaos*, London: Penguin (US edition, Simon and Schuster, 1992).

Wiggins, S. (1990): *An Introduction to Applied Nonlinear Dynamical Systems and Chaos*, New York: Springer-Verlag.

Williamson, O.E. (1975): *Markets and Hierarchies: Analysis and Antitrust Implications*, New York: Free Press.

Williamson, O.E., and S.G. Winter (eds.) (1991): *The Nature of the Firm: Origins, Evolution and Development*, Cambridge: Cambridge University Press.

Wiseman, J. (ed.) (1983): *Beyond Positive Economics?*, London: Macmillan.

Witt, U. (1991): 'Turning Austrian Economics into an Evolutionary Theory', in B. Caldwell and S. Boehm (eds.), *Austrian Economics: Tensions and New Developments*, Boston, Mass.: Kluwer Academic Press.

Zarnowitz, V. (1985): 'Recent Work on Business Cycles in Historical Perspective', *Journal of Economic Literature*, Vol.23, pp.523-80.

Zimmerman, B. (1992): *Chaos and Self-Renewing Organizations: Designing Transformation Processes for Co-Evolution*, Working Paper 29-92, Faculty of Administration, Ontario, Canada: York University.

Zimmerman, B., and D.K. Hurst (1992): *Breaking the Boundaries: the Fractal Organization*, Working Paper 309-92, Faculty of Administration, Ontario, Canada: York University.